# AMERICAN ADVERTISING

GARLAND REFERENCE LIBRARY
OF SOCIAL SCIENCE
(Vol. 398)

# AMERICAN ADVERTISING
*A Reference Guide*

Emelda L. Williams, Ph.D.
*and*
Donald W. Hendon, Ph.D.

GARLAND PUBLISHING, INC. • NEW YORK & LONDON
1988

© 1988 Emelda L. Williams and Donald W. Hendon
All rights reserved

Library of Congress Cataloging-in-Publication Data
Williams, Emelda L., 1937–
American advertising: a reference guide/Emelda L. Williams and
Donald W. Hendon.
p.cm.—(Garland reference library of social science; vol. 398)
Bibliography: p.
Includes index.
ISBN 0–8240–8490–X (alk. paper)
1. Advertising—United States—Bibliography. I. Hendon, Donald W. II. Title. III. Series: Garland reference library of social science; v. 398.
Z7164.C81W55 1988 [HF5823] 016.6591'0973—dc19
87-32148 CIP

Printed on acid-free, 250-year-life paper
Manufactured in the United States of America

CONTENTS

Introduction                                              vii

Chapter I: Advertising Overview                             1

   A. History of Advertising                               4
   B. Theoretical Issues, Cases and Research             12
   C. Ethical, Economic and Social Issues                22
   D. Motivation and Psychological Issues                34
   E. Reference Guides                                   41
   F. Professional Journals and Periodicals              49
   G. Advertising Texts                                  57

Chapter II: The Institution of Advertising                 67

   A. Advertising Agencies                               69
   B. Suppliers                                          80
   C. Media                                              83
      1. Media Planning and Selection                   83
      2. Print Media                                    94
      3. Electronic Media                              103
      4. Direct Marketing and Out-of-Home Media        118
      5. Sales Promotion and Supplementary Media       125

Chapter III: Creating the Advertising — 135

    A. Creativity — 137
    B. Production — 143
    C. Layout and Copy Writing — 151
    D. Art and Visual — 159

Chapter IV: Special Types of Advertising — 163

    A. Local Advertising — 165
    B. Corporate Advertising and Public Relations — 170
    C. Noncommercial and Political Advertising — 178
    D. International Advertising — 184
    E. Professional and Services Advertising — 193
    F. Advertising Classics — 197

Author Index — 201

# INTRODUCTION

What you are about to read is a compilation of the most important articles and books in the field of American advertising published in the last twenty years or so. These articles and books have been summarized for you, but the summaries are not so succinct that you don't know what's in them. You will be able to tell rather quickly, and this means you will know right way, whether you want to find the original book or article and dig more deeply into the information contained there. In other words, this is a reference book on reference books and reference articles that most advertising and marketing executives need to be familiar with if they want to stay on top of their profession. It is advertising's "common body of knowledge"—and then some.

The books and articles contain some old classics dating back to the early 1900's, as well as the latest writings by practitioners and academics. They were chosen with you, the reader, in mind. We wanted to give you something to help you in your job—a time-saving tool to get ahead in your career. For example, media buyers will find material on advertising media—the long forgotten media that were hot in the years past (such as signboard over shops) as well as the latest in technological innovations. Likewise, creative types such as copywriters will find what they're looking for. Generalists and managers will find books and articles they will want to read, too.

For academics—especially those engaged in research-this annotated bibliography will save you a lot of time and money. Get the title from the university computer and read the description here.

In short, we have written this annotated bibliography with the reader in mind. "User-friendly" is an over used term in the late 1980's, but we feel that our compilation is just that—user-friendly in the most helpful sense. There are 24 major headings, which we feel cover everything that readers in the advertising world deal with every day and want to know more about. Not only do we have many books and articles that are primarily related to each of the 24 categories, we have cross-referenced books and articles that fit into more than one category. For example, under media planning and selection, we have 42 primary sources, along with 12 from some of the other 23 categories that also have a bearing on media planning and selection.

This reference book concerns itself primarily with American advertising, not with advertising in other nations. However, there is a section on international advertising that is a springboard for a future reference book. We feel that advertising practitioners and scholars in other nations will get a lot of value out of our compilation, since the American advertising industry is recognized as a leader throughout the world. Other nations can learn from the unique American experience in advertising.

Our reference guide to American advertising contains four chapters—(1) Advertising Overview, with seven sections, (2) Institutions of Advertising, with seven sections, (3) Creating the Advertising, with four sections, and (4) Special Types of Advertising, with six sections.

Of course, any classification scheme is arbitrary. It can oversimplify, distort, or omit—as does any theory. We had many long discussions in which we exchanged opinions in an open and frank manner, trying to come up with the outline you will see on the Contents page. And we had even more, longer discussions, as to what books and articles should be included and which should be omitted in keeping with the constraints imposed upon us. We asked the advice of many others in our field, both practitioners and academicians, and you are about to read the results. Compromises had to be made, and we take full responsibility for any omissions—or for items we included which you think should not have been. You are our customers, and being marketing oriented, we both know how important customers are. You readers are marketing oriented, too. We all practice the marketing concept. So please give us your feedback before we start on the second edition. Thanks, we hope you enjoy the results of our efforts as much as we enjoyed compiling everything. We look forward to hearing from you with your suggestions and comments.

Special thanks go to those who assisted with the typing and other clerical work: Kathy Dawson and Varonica Wilson. Of course, without the diligent research efforts of our graduate student, James Philpot, this work would have taken much longer to complete. James brought his experience with a B.S. in English and M.B.A. to do a terrific job in editing and understanding advertising issues and concepts.

Our spouses, Dr. Bill Williams, and Mrs. Rebecca Hendon, gave us moral support when it was needed the most. We thank them with our love.

Emelda L. Williams, Ph.D.
Donald W. Hendon, Ph.D.

# CHAPTER ONE

# ADVERTISING OVERVIEW

# ADVERTISING OVERVIEW

Promotional strategy plays a significant role in marketing; that is, the creation of mutually beneficial exchanges between producers and consumers of goods, services, and ideas. Promotion is one part of the marketing mix, and advertising is one part of the promotional mix. Personal selling, sales promotion, public relations, and packaging are also parts of the promotional mix.

This reference guide deals mainly with advertising, which is a paid form of nonpersonal communication usually persuasive in nature about products, services and ideas by an identified sponsor to a specific target market. Sales promotion and public relations are also a part of this reference guide.

In the first chapter, there are annotated references on the history of advertising, theoretical issues, cases, research, ethical, economic, social, motivation, and psycho-logical issues. In addition, a listing of various articles and books that can serve as a reference guide is included. A detailed, but not comprehensive, list of advertising journals and periodicals is also listed. Some of the text-books that are used in the academic setting are annotated.

## History of Advertising

As the world's industrial output has grown, so has the use of advertising. Throughout history, the purpose of advertising—to inform, persuade and remind—has not changed. However, many events occurred in the United States that changed the course of advertising: the invention of new ways of printing and photography, the worldwide Industrial Revolution, the rise of the broadcast industry, and changing social and cultural mores. This section includes annotated articles in such areas as anthology of advertising authors, historical presentations, and an overview of advertising as it has evolved over the years.

1. Abrahams, Howard P. "Retail Advertising: Radio Break-Through in the 60's; TV in the 70's." *Television/Radio Age*. 21 November 1983: 222-224.

   Discusses the growth in the use of radio and television advertising during the 1960's and 1970's.Several case histories of successful campaigns are recalled, and the many improvements in radio-televisionproduction techniques that occurred during this period are discussed.

2. Assael, Henry, and C. Samuel Craig, editors. *The History of Advertising*. New York: Garland Publishing, Inc., 1985.

   A forty-volume facsimile series of major books on advertising. Books by various authors are organized into sections on: history, psychology, advertising management, economic and social aspects of advertising, the agency, creativity, evaluation, media, biographies and specialized areas.

3. Belk, Russell W., and Richard W. Pollary. "Images of Ourselves: The Good Life in Twentieth Century Advertising." *Journal of Consumer Research.* 11 (1984-1985): 887-897.

   Presents the results of a content analysis of U.S. magazine advertisements between 1900 and 1980. The authors conclude that advertising through the years may have portrayed a progressively more luxurious lifestyle and that recent advertising portrays consumption as an end in itself rather than a means to consumer satisfaction.

4. Calkins, Earnest Elmo, and Ralph Holden. *Modern Advertising.* New York: Garland Publishing, Inc., 1985. Reprint.

   This turn-of-the-century advertising handbook includes all aspects of the field of advertising. Topics discussed include print and outdoor advertising, the advertising manager and agency, retail and mail order advertising and copy layout. The authors include illustrations and examples in their discussion.

5. Cohen, Dorothy. *Advertising.* New York: John Wiley and Sons, Inc., 1972.

   A comprehensive text, *Advertising* discusses the history of advertising, the advertising agency, creativity and media. The book examines advertising as a part of the marketing mix and an element of the promotion process.

6. Dyer, Gillian. *Advertising as Communication.* London: Methuen & Co. Ltd., 1982.

   This book discusses advertising as a vital form of social communication that influences our thoughts and lives. Discusses the history of advertising, its effects, its meanings, the media, and the language and rhetoric of advertising.

7. *50 Years of Advertising as Seen Through the Eyes of Advertising Age.* Chicago: Crain Books, 1987.

6  American Advertising

Presents photos, ads, and news clips from award-winning campaigns that were documented in *Advertising Age*. Arranged by decade and color coded for easy reference.

8. Fleming, Thomas. "How It Was in Advertising: 1776-1976." *Advertising Age*. 19 April 1976: 1, 27-35.

This historical presentation notes the influences of men such as Ben Franklin, Paul Revere, and George Washington on Advertising during the Civil War, the development of outdoor advertising, and consumerism in the Depression are all given special attention. Also, a bicentennial collection of advertisements is presented.

9. Green, Norma F. "Unusual Media Through the Years." *SCAN* (condensed from *Adweek/Midwest*) November, 1985: 21-2.

Briefly surveys the history of outdoor advertising and includes accounts of several unusual outdoor advertisements.

10. Griese, Noel L. "AT&T: 1908 Origins of the Nation's Oldest Continuous Institutional Advertising Campaign." *Journal of Advertising*. Summer 1977: 18-23.

This article studies the institutional advertising of AT&T from 1908 to 1975. It gives a historical review of the animosity toward AT&T in its early years, as well as a look at Theodore N. Vail, then president of AT&T. Also included are the five original ads prepared for AT&T by N. W. Ayer Agency.

11. Griffith, Robert. "The Selling of America: The Advertising Council and American Politics. 1942-1960." *Business History Review*. 57 (1983): 388-412.

Traces the development and positions taken by the Ad Council in its early years. Initially formed to combat the anti-corporatism of the 1930's, the council has become a strong force often strongly supporting or opposing the policies of presidential administrations. The council is most famous for its millions of public service announcements and promoting the advertising industry.

12. Henry, Brian, editor. *British Television Advertising: The First Thirty Years*. London: History of Advertising Trust, 1986.

    A year-by-year history of advertising on Independent Television in Britain from 1955 to 1985. The book discusses how outside events influenced and were influenced by ITV. The creative development of advertising, production, advertising agencies, and great television commercials are also discussed.

13. Hopkins, Claude. *Scientific Advertising*. New York: Crown Publishers, Inc., 1966.

    A 1923 classic on advertising has been reprinted with 21 concise chapters dealing mainly on how to write advertising copy.

14. Johnson, J. Douglas. *Advertising Today*. Chicago: Science Research Association, Inc., 1978.

    This introductory text attempts to provide a "real world" perspective, emphasizing the practice of advertising. Especially strong are the discussions of the history of advertising and creativity.

* *Journal of Advertising History*. Bradford, England. Cited as item 178.

15. Kenner, H. J. *The Fight for Truth in Advertising*. New York: Garland Publishing, Inc., 1985. Reprint.

    Kenner, a leader in the formation and development of the Better Business Bureau, describes early incidents of deceptive advertising and chronicles the crusade for truth in advertising.

16. Larwood, Jacob and John Camden Hotten. *The History of Signboards from the Earliest Times*. London: Chatto and Windus, 1898.

This early book focuses on signs, especially wood-carved tavern signs, and includes many illustrations, anecdotes and explanations of symbols.

17. Leachman, Harden Bryant. *The Early Advertising Scene.* New York: Garland Publishing, Inc., Reprint. 1985.

    An early twentieth century advertising agent recounts the nature and conditions of advertising in the years prior to federal regulation.

18. Lewis, E. St. Elmo. *Financial Advertising, For Commercial and Savings Banks, Trust Title Insurance, and Safe Deposit Companies, Investment Houses.* New York: Garland Publishing, Inc., 1985. Reprint.

    Discusses the history of advertising from the ancient Greeks to advertising in early America and the production of advertisements for the highly regulated financial industry. The author discusses the banker's ethical duty to the public and the special problems of financial advertising.

19. Lipstein, Benjamin. "A Historical Retrospective of Copy Research." *Journal of Advertising Research.* New York: Advertising Research Foundation. December 1984/January 1985: 11-14.

    Lipstein briefly reviews the history of copy research and the various types and techniques of copy research, concluding that the copy research field is a dynamic one. Day-after-recall, motivation research, the theater technique, and the ASI graphic technique are discussed.

20. Marchand, Lowland. *Advertising the American Dream: Making Way for Modernity, 1920-1940.* Los Angeles: University of California Press, 1985.

    The author describes and analyzes advertisements and ad campaigns from the period, 1920-1940, arguing that the advertisements were not indicative of reality in the average situations of behavior in the nation. The period's advertising, however, made the sweeping social changes of the 1920's-30's more acceptable.

21. Nevett, T. R. *Advertising in Britain—A History.* Bradford, England: MCB University Press, 1982.

    Discusses the development of advertising as a business tool in Great Britain from before the Industrial Revolution to the present. The focus is on the advertisers, their techniques, their products, and the public. Extensively illustrated.

22. *Papers of The American Association of Advertising Agencies.* New York: Garland Publishing, Inc., 1985. Reprint.

    A series of essays describing in great detail various aspects of advertising including copy writing, media selection, research, graphics and business management. Also includes the Association Research Department's assessment of magazine readership in the 1920's.

23. Pease, Otis A. "Advertising Ethics," *Arizona Review*, October 1969: 1-5.

    The author analyzes the development of the ethical standards of advertising and gives a brief history of advertising ethics. He compares advertising with other institutions and explains that advertising cannot be concerned with controversial political and religious issues.

24. Perlongo, Bob, editor. *Early American Advertising.* New York: Art Direction Book Company, 1985.

    A collection of over 200 advertisements from signboards, bills, and newspapers is presented. Dating from 1799 to 1924, these classic advertisements sell every type of product (legitimate and illegitimate) imaginable. Many of the ads are briefly reviewed.

10   American Advertising

\*   Peterson, R. D. "The Evolution of Advertising Agency Services." Cited as item 298.

25. Pollary, Richard W. "The Subsidizing Sizzle: A Descriptive History of Print Advertising, 1900-1980." *Journal of Marketing* Summer 1985: 24-37.

    Reviews the content and techniques of advertising from 1900 to 1980 by analyzing the content of 2000 magazine ads. A decade-by-decade analysis reveals the popular fads and trends in print advertising style and technique.

26. Presbrey, Frank. *The History and Development of Advertising.* Garden City, New York: Doubleday, 1929.

    An early history of advertising, this account begins in the ancient world and traces the development of advertising through English and American history. This comprehensive work contains many illustrations of advertisements, especially nineteenth-century print advertising. Anachronisms throughout the book (one section is entitled "Some Effects of the World War on Advertising") make it of historical interest.

27. *Printer's Ink. Fifty Years 1888-1938.* New York: Garland Publishing, Inc., 1986. Reprint.

    The fiftieth year anniversary issue of *Printer's Ink*, the first periodical concerned solely with marketing, is devoted to a review of the events of the advertising world from 1888 to 1938. Original advertisements are included.

28. Serafin, Raymond. "Flourishing Roman Ad Biz Found," *Advertising Age.* May 16, 1986: 1, 93.

    Reports on research into the history of advertising in ancient Rome. A study shows that Roman advertising was prominent and used many techniques popular today. Popular Roman techniques included branding, product positioning, and endorsements by athletes and other famous figures.

29. Wheeler, Elmer. *Tested Sentences That Sell.* Englewood Cliffs, New Jersey: Prentice-Hall, Inc., 1937.

Valuable to today's student for its historical viewpoint, this 1937 book teaches selling techniques that have been adapted to many copywriting and salesmanship texts today as used by door-to-door salepeople.

30. Wright, John W. *The Commercial Connection—Advertising and the American Mass Media.* New York: Dell, 1979.

This text supplement contains 35 readings dealing with advertising issues, audiences, and history. Also included is an appendix with statistics on advertisers, advertising agencies, rates, and expenditures.

## Theoretical Issues, Cases and Research

A systematic approach to promotional planning and strategy is important to the advertiser. By analyzing theoretical issues, cases and secondary research, much information can be gleaned. This section highlights some articles and books on such topics as: how to establish advertising budgets, analyze quantitative and qualitative models for use in advertising, effectiveness of advertising, and useful cases for classroom or training use. Results of many research efforts are also annotated.

31. Aaker, David A., Editor. *Advertising Management.* Englewood Cliffs, New Jersey: Prentice-Hall, Inc., 1975.

    This collection of 48 previously published readings in advertising management covers the advertising process, setting advertising objectives, the communication process, media decisions, and legal, economic and social issues.

32. Aaker, David A., and John G. Myers. *Advertising Management.* Englewood Cliffs, New Jersey: Prentice-Hall, Inc., 1982.

    This text combines the qualitative and behavioral elements of advertising with the quantitative models of statistics and management science in an investigation of decision making in the mass media. The six parts of the book discuss the historical perspective of advertising, setting advertising objectives, communication models, copy decisions, media decisions, and social issues. A good source book for the advertising manager.

33. Acito, Franklin, and Jeffery D. Ford. "How Advertising Affects Employees," *Business Horizons.* 23 (February 1980): 53-59.

The authors use case studies to examine the effect of advertising on employees of the firm—a not often considered audience.

34. Advertising Research Foundation. *Copy Testing: A Study Prepared for the Advertising Research Foundation.* New York: Garland Publishing, Inc., 1985. Reprint.

    This book discusses the various copy testing practices used in the 1930's, including opinion tests, recognition tests, recall tests, coupon tests and sales tests. The uses, advantages, and disadvantages of each test method are discussed

35. Berg, Gerald C. *The Incumbency Reinforcement Theory of Advertising and Profitability.* Ph.D. dissertation. University of Maryland, 1984.

    Offers a theory to explain the much-observed correlation between advertising and profitability. Advertising influences brand loyalty in consumers. Early market entrants advertise to reinforce loyalty, and later entrants advertise to break brand loyalty. Complications of this theory are tested empirically.

36. Bernhardt, Kenneth L., and Thomas C. Kinnear. *Cases in Marketing Management.* Third Edition. Homewood, Illinois: Business Publications, Inc., 1986.

    Includes ten cases dealing with promotion decisions.

37. Boyd, Harper W. Jr., Vernon Fryburger, and Ralph Westfall. *Cases in Advertising Management.* New York: McGraw-Hill Book Company, 1964.

    This casebook is a set of reasonably short, analytical studies of problems commonly faced by agency personnel and their clients in creativity, media and promotion decisions, and management of the advertising department and agency.

38. Burton, Phillip Ward, and Richard Sandhusen. *Cases in Advertising.* Columbus, Ohio: Grid Publishing, Inc., 1981.

This casebook presents a series of short cases that can be used to supplement textbook concepts with real-life experiences.

39. Dirksen, Charles J., Arthur Kroeger, and Franco M. Nicosia. *Advertising: Principles and Management Cases.* Sixth Edition. Homewood, Illinois: Richard D. Irwin, Inc., 1984.

    Case-study text focuses on the decision-making processes of management in the use of advertising within the marketing mix. Fifty-four cases reinforce learning in the areas of advertising management, communication processes, creativity, media decisions, economic, social, and legal issues.

40. Duetsch, Larry L. "Advertising and Profitability Among Large Industrial Corporations," *Quarterly Review of Economics and Business.* Winter 1982: 81-88.

    Seeks to evaluate the impact of television advertising as compared with other media by comparing the advertising/profits relationships of corporations that use television with those corporations not using television. No significant differences between the relationships are found, but profitability was found to vary directly with the amount spent on advertising.

41. Engel, James F., and W. Wayne Talarzyk. *Cases in Promotional Strategy*, Revised Edition. Homewood, Illinois: Richard D. Irwin, Inc., 1984.

    Features actual current cases in promotion of both profit and nonprofit organizations. Cases are divided into four areas: planning, managing mass communications, personal selling, and stimulating reseller support.

42. Engel, James F., Martin R. Warshaw, and Thomas C. Kinnear. *Promotional Strategy.* Sixth Edition. Homewood, Illinois: Richard D. Irwin, Inc., 1987.

    This text is a comprehensive coverage of promotional strategy. Included are discussions of consumer psychology, promotion objectives, advertising management, reseller support, promotion coordination, and socioeconomic impact of promotion.

43. Finn, David W. "The Integrated Information Response Model," *Journal of Advertising* 13 (1, 1984): 24-33.

    Evaluates the conditions under which advertising may have a direct impact upon consumer attitude within the context of two consumer behavior models.

44. Gardner, Burleigh B. *A Conceptual Framework for Advertising*. Chicago: Crain Books, 1983.

    Designed to be the first step in instituting an ongoing dialogue between educational leaders and advertising practitioners. Advertisers and agencies are provided an outline for improvement of advertising efforts and more accurate predictions of outcomes.

45. Gelb, Betsy D., and Charles M. Pickett. "Attitude-toward-the-Ad: Links to Humor and to Advertising Effectiveness." *Journal of Advertising* 12 (2, 1983): 34-42.

    Studies the impact of humor on favorable attitudes toward advertisements. Concludes that humor may aid advertising effectiveness, but the relationship is moderated by the consumer's attitudes toward the ad.

46. Ghosh, Avijit, and C. Samuel Craig, editors. *The Relationship of Advertising Expenditures to Sales: An Anthology of Classic Articles*. New York: Garland Publishing, Inc., 1985.

    Contains articles which document the relationship of advertising expenditures to sales. The articles deal both with the overall market and particular brands.

47. Grossbart, Sanford, Darrel D. Muehling, and Norman Kaugun. "Verbal and Visual References to Competition in Comparative Advertising," *Journal of Advertising* 15 (1, 1986): 10-23.

Contrasts the effects of comparative and noncomparative print advertisements, focusing on cognitive, affective, and behaviorial reactions to the advertisements. Finds that the advantages and disadvantages of each format depend upon the advertisers' objectives.

48. *HBR Reprints: Advertising.* Cambridge, Massachusetts: Harvard Business School Publishing Division, 1986.

   Eight articles reprinted from the *Harvard Business Review* investigate new techniques and technologies for reaching customers through advertising.

49. Hendon, Donald W. and Emelda L. Williams. "Winning the Battle for Your Customer," *Journal of Consumer Marketing.* 2 (Fall 1985): 65-75.

   Segmenting the market by the dimension personality, psychographics and positioning is the thrust of this article. Examples of advertising illustrate how to use those three "P's" with the conventional 4 "P's" of the marketing mix. Advertising helps to win the battle of the customer's mind.

50. Jones, John Philip. *What's in a Name?* Lexington, Massachusetts: Lexington Books, 1986.

   Discusses branding and argues that the purpose of advertising is the reinforcement of brand loyalty. The factors that shape a brand through each stage of its life cycle are discussed as are advertising strategies which incorporate these factors. Jones also explains creativity in branding campaigns.

\*   *Journal of Advertising Research.* Advertising Research Foundation. Cited as item 179.

51. Kohn, Paul M., Reginald G. Smart, and Alan C. Ogbourne. "Effects of Two Kinds of Alcohol Advertising on Subsequent Consumption." *Journal of Advertising* 13 (1, 1984): 34-40, 48.

Reports the results of a survey to determine the effects of "lifestyle" and "tombstone" advertisements on consumption of alcohol. Neither kind of ad was found to have an effect on immediate or delayed consumption, and the ads' evaluations showed no significant difference.

\* Lipstein, Benjamin. "An Historical Retrospective of Copy Research." Cited above as item 20.

52. Nichols, Len M. "Advertising and Economic Welfare," *American Economic Review*. 75 (1985): 213-218.

    Examines advertising expenditures and attempts to develop a theoretical model for determining the social optimality of advertising.

53. Nylen, David W. *Advertising: Planning, Implementation, and Control*, Third Edition. Cincinnati, Ohio: South-Western, 1986.

    An advertising management text which presents, in separate units, an overview of advertising, analysis of consumer needs, the budgeting, creative, and production processes, and the evaluation of campaigns. This edition is updated to include discussions on modern electronic media, technological advances in production processes, and the legal and regulatory environments.

54. Oshikawa, Sadaomi and John J. Wheatley. "Learning Theory, Attitudes and Advertising," *University of Washington Business Review*. Summer 1968: 24-33.

    A summary of applications of contemporary learning theory to advertising is presented in this article. The implications for marketing are discussed in relation to stimulus-response contiguity, stimulus response reinforcement, and cognitive and operant-conditioning theories. The contribution of the cognitive approach to theory of attitude change and structure is thoroughly discussed.

55. Pasadeos, Yorga. "A Bibliometric Study of Advertising Citations," 14(4, 1985): 52-59.

    Examines the citations in advertising literature to determine the major sources for advertising research. Business and psychology publications accounted for over half the citations during the period 1981-83. The relative impact of individual advertising publications is assessed.

56. Percy, Larry, and Arch G. Woodside. *Advertising and Consumer Psychology*. Lexington, Massachusetts: Lexington Books, Spring 1986.

    Deals with modern developments of advertising theory and research methods. It also shows how these theories can affect contemporary advertising strategies.

57. Picquet, Sylvere. "The Role of Advertising in the Marketing Mix." *European Research*. March 1979: 82-89.

    Examines the individual parts of advertising in order to clarify any ambiguities that exist between advertising and sales promotion. Ways of setting budgets reviewed as well as expenditure accounting procedures and assessing effectiveness.

58. Preston, Ivan L. "The Association Model of the Advertising Communication Process," *Journal of Advertising* 11 (2, 1982): 3-15.

    Presents a new advertising process model based upon various predecessor models. The Association Model incorporates elements of research and theory from AIDA, S-R psychology, and consumer information processing. The author also reviews literature on the function of association in advertising.

59. Ring, Lawrence J., Derek A. Newton, Neil H. Bordon and E. Ralph Biggadike. *Decisions In Marketing: Cases and Text*. Homewood, Illinois: Business Publications Inc., 1986.

A decision-oriented marketing management casebook containing thirty-seven cases. Although the book deals mainly with marketing in general, several cases focus specifically on advertising.

60. Roman, Kenneth, and Jane Maas. *How to Advertise.* New York: St. Martins Press, 1976.

    Two agency executives build upon advertising principles and experience in explaining how to conceive, develop, and produce sound advertising campaigns. Chapters discuss product positioning, the best strategies for the various media, ad production, advertisement testing, truth in advertising, and advertiser/agency relations.

61. Rossiter, John R., and Larry Percy. *Advertising and Promotion Management.* New York: McGraw-Hill, 1987.

    A text in promotional management which emphasizes the communications function of promotion. All the standard topics in advertising and promotion management are covered with emphases on choosing the proper communication model for a particular product or brand.

62. Rotzoll, Kim B., James E. Haefner, and Charles H. Sandage. *Advertising in Contemporary Society: Perspectives Toward Understanding.* Cincinnati, Ohio: South Western, 1986.

    Explores current social topics in advertising such as the media and advertising, ethics, regulation, and economics. Highly theoretical.

63. Sawyer, Howard G. *Business-to-Business Advertising: How to Compete for a $1-Trillion-Plus Market.* Chicago: Crain books, 1983.

    All basic elements from advertising strategy development to result measurement and testing are covered in this book. This book is written from a pragmatic viewpoint.

64. Scheuing, Eberhard E. "Advertising That Sells," *Marketing Journal.* No. 2, 1976: 176-178.

   Analyzes an advertisement published by Ogilvy and Mather. He groups the Ogilvy and Mather suggestions into eight categories which are outlined in this article. Also, the author reviews the advertising situation in America and how it is different from the European situation.

65. Scott, Walter Dill. *The Theory of Advertising: A Simple Exposition of The Principles of Psychology in Their Relation to Successful Advertising.* New York, Garland Publishing, Inc., 1985. Reprint.

   One of the early works about the psychology of advertising, this book focuses on the communication process and problems of attention and perception and how these principles can be applied to advertising problems.

66. Stanley, Richard E. *Promotion: Advertising, Publicity, Personal Selling, Sales Promotion.* Englewood Cliffs, New Jersey: Prentice-Hall, 1977.

   This text focuses primarily on the theoretical basics of promotion. The specifics of promotional techniques are avoided in favor of the broader discussion of the "promotion process." Gives good insight into the concerns and activities of the promotional manager.

67. Tauber, Edward M. "Editorial: How Does Advertising Work?" *Journal of Advertising Research.* December 1982/January 1983: 7.

   Reviews the various theories of how advertising works and which variables influence advertisement effectiveness. Theories mentioned include AIDA, DAGMAR, attitude change theories, reinforcement theories, and agenda setting theories. Appropriate situations for each theory are described.

68. Watkins, Julian Lewis. *The 100 Greatest Advertisements*. New York: Dover Publications, Inc., Reprinted 1986.

    Traces the history of some of the most effective ads ever printed. It reveals selling clues, ideas and key facts. This volume is a good reference for effective advertising.

69. Zacher, Robert V. *Advertising Techniques and Management*. Revised edition. Homewood, Illinois: Richard D. Irwin, Inc., 1967.

    Examines the role of advertising in product distribution and seeks to give an appreciation of the communication function of advertising. Creativity and production are discussed in addition to advertising and media management.

## Ethical, Economic and Social Issues

Because advertising publicly invites people to try certain products, it is often criticized for the way it influences our society. Environmental scanning is a way of developing an understanding of the influences that impact on the consumer. Ethical, economic and social issues are highlighted in this section.

70. Abernethy, Avery M. and Jesse E. Teel. "Advertising Regulation's Effect upon Demand for Cigarettes." *Journal of Advertising* 15(4,1968): 51-5.

    Examines the possible impact of proposed additional regulation of tobacco and alcoholic beverage advertising. This examination is based on the effect that advertising regulation has had on tobacco consumption in the past.

\*   Acito, Franklin and Jeffery D. Ford. "How Advertising Affects Employees." Cited above as item 33.

71. "Advertising and the Corrupting of America," *Business and Society Review.* Spring 1982: 64-69.

    Advertising industry leaders and observers respond to an economist's prior claim that advertising is the "deadliest subversive force within capitalism." A majority of the respondents disagree strongly, citing advertising's information quality and its contribution to individual and economic freedom.

72. Barbour, Frederic L., II and David M. Gardner. "Deceptive Advertising: A Practical Approach to Measurement," *Journal of Advertising* 11 (1, 1982): 21-30.

Presents a simple methodology for detecting and measuring deception in advertisements, using the impressions of subjects exposed to the ads rather than the opinions of "experts." Specific findings of price deception in newspaper advertising are presented.

73. Barnes, Judith A. *Gender Portrayal in Magazine Advertising.* Ph.D. dissertation. Rensselaer Polytechnic Institute, 1984.

    Examines advertising in various types of magazines in the years 1953, 1979, and 1983 in order to determine trends in sex-stereotyping in advertisements. Finds that over the thirty years, portrayals have become less stereotypical, but from 1979 to 1983 the portrayals of gender have become more traditional.

74. Bartone, Nicholas Michael. *The Effect of Self-Regulation on the Ethical Conduct of TV Drug Advertising—1973 to 1983.* Ph.D. Dissertation, University of Minnesota, 1986.

    Studies television advertisements for over-the-counter drugs for years between 1973 and 1983 which represent periods of varying self-regulation. Pharmacy and medical students rate the commercials' ethical conduct. The commercials are found to be "fair" but less than acceptable for all years.

\* Berg, Gerald C. *The Incumbency Reinforcement Theory of Advertising and Profitability.* Cited above as item 35.

75. Bloom, Paul N. "Effective Marketing for Professional Services." *Harvard Business Review.* September-October 1984: 102-110.

    Discusses the need for marketing of professional services and the problems associated with professional marketing. Marketing challenges and suggestions for resolving them are given. They include: ethical and legal constraints, buyer uncertainty, need to be perceived as having experience, limited differentiability, immeasurable benefits of advertising, converting "doers" into "sellers," and allocating time for marketing.

76. Bullard, Jerri Hayes. *Professionals' Attitudes Toward Advertising: A Study of Lawyers, Dentists and Accountants*. Ph.D. dissertation. Virginia Polytechnic Institute and State University, 1983.

   Surveys accountants, lawyers and dentists to find professionals' perceptions of advertising. The factors influencing professionals' attitudes are analyzed, and attitudes of professionals toward advertising are found to be best explained by occupation and city of practice.

77. Cherington, Paul Terry. *The Consumer Looks at Advertising*. New York: Garland Publishing, Inc., 1985. Reprint.

   Suggests that consumers like to buy brand-name merchandise and that advertising will increase the consumption of higher quality goods at the expense of lower-quality goods. In this 1928 book, the author also promotes advertising of professional services.

78. Cohen, Dorothy. "Legal Interpretations of Deception Are Deceiving." *Marketing News*. September 26, 1986: 12-13.

   Reviews the Federal Trade Commission's standard for deciding whether advertising is deceptive. The definition, "tendency or capacity to deceive" is ambiguous, and recent court decisions have added further ambiguity, causing problems for advertisers.

79. Courtney, Alice E., and Thomas W. Whipple. *Sex Stereotyping in Advertising*. Lexington, Massachusetts: Lexington Books, 1986.

   Examines the media's handling of sex roles in advertising and gives suggestions for producing more effective, less offensive advertisements.

80. Diamond, Sidney A. *Trademark Problems and How to Avoid Them*. Revised edition. Chicago: Crain Books, 1983.

Diamond, a former U.S. Commissioner of Patents and Trademarks, discusses problems which can arise in the selection and protection of trademarks and in comparative or imitative advertising. Techniques for avoiding problems are suggested.

81. Durand, Richard M., and Zarrel V. Lambert. "Alienation and Criticisms of Advertising." *Journal of Advertising* 14 (3, 1985): 9-17.

Proposes the hypothesis that advertising criticisms arise from consumer and political alienation rather than the shortcomings of advertising practices. Implies that managers have the potential to increase advertising effectiveness and efficiency while reducing criticism and alienation in the environment.

82. Freeman, Alan. "Quebec Law Protecting Kids from Ads Rankles Companies." *Wall Street Journal.* December 19, 1985: 23.

This article discusses Canadian firms' reactions to a law which bans advertising aimed to children under thirteen. Companies are severely hampered by having to shift the focus of their advertisements to an older audience.

83. French, George. *Advertising: The Social and Economic Problem.* New York: Garland Publishing, Inc., 1985. Reprint.

A revealing look at advertising in the beginning of the century, the author examines the issues of advertising ethics and the social effects of advertising.

84. Geller, Max A. *Advertising at the Crossroads: Federal Regulation vs. Voluntary Controls.* New York: Garland Publishing, Inc., 1985. Reprint.

Considers the advertising industry's potential for deception and the consequences of deceptive advertising. The growth of federal regulatory agencies is discussed, and the author advocates voluntary controls in order to avoid regulation.

85. Glessing, Robert J., and William P. White. *Mass Media: The Invisible Environment.* Chicago: Science Research Associates, Inc., 1973.

A collection of essays which discuss the extent to which the mass media affect and shape the lives of the public. The authors' purpose is to help the reader to control and use information from the media rather than be manipulated by the media.

86. Greyser, Stephen A. "Advertising: Attacks & Counters," *Harvard Business Review.* March-April 1972: 22-28.

Discusses the social criticisms of advertising with regard to ability to influence, taste, information content, and impact on social values. He categorizes advertisers based on these points and offers suggestions for advertisers to follow in order to avoid criticism and regulation.

87. Griffin, George. "Laissez-Faire Advertising." *Graphic Arts Monthly.* October 1985: 180-82.

Discusses several ethical issues in advertising, including the increased use of "negative option" promotions and the word "free" in advertisements. The author concludes that laissez-faire might be a good policy because the most effective ads, according to his experience, simply tell the truth in a creative way.

88. Gross, Micheal. "Sex Sells." *Saturday Review.* July/ August 1985: 50-52, 91.

Discusses the magazine industry's increased use of sex and sex-related topics in order to sell copies. Magazines mentioned in the article include: *Playboy, Newsweek, GQ, Mademoiselle, New Republic, Sports Illustrated,* and others.

89. Harms, John B. *Advertising Communication in the United States: Information or Persuasion?* Ph.D. Dissertation, University of Kansas, 1985.

Examines the traditional arguments for and against advertising. Surveys industry members perceptions of advertising as a form of communication and how external, social structural factors shape decisions to inform and persuade.

90. Hulbert, James. "Advertising: Criticism and Reply," *Business and Society*. Autumn 1965: 33-42.

    Discusses arguments that advertising is deliberately misrepresenting, vulgar, culturally distasteful, and manipulative. The author holds that if advertising were distasteful, it would not promote business goals. He also warns that advertising should be ethical if businesses are to maintain their freedom.

91. "Image of Advertising." *Editor and Publisher*. February 9, 1985: 15, 32.

    Discusses the American Association of Advertising Agencies' print and campaign aimed at improving the image of advertising. The ads focus on dispelling myths about advertising such as the myths that advertising raises the cost of goods, and advertising can make consumers purchase products they don't want.

\*   Kenner, H. J. The Fight for Truth in Advertising. Cited above as item 15.

92. Kirkpatrick, Jerry. "A Philosophic Defense of Advertising." *Journal of Advertising* 15 (2, 1986): 42-48, 64.

    Presents a non-traditional defense of advertising based on the premise that it is morally right to do what is in one's self-interest. The author argues that charges against advertising result from a hostility toward capitalism.

93. Kunkel, Dale Lyman. *Children's Understanding of Television Advertising: The Impact of Host-Selling*. Ph.D. dissertation. University of Southern California, 1984.

Examines the effects of host-selling on children. Host-selling occurs when advertisement content features the same characters as the adjacent program content. Kunkel finds that with host-selling children have difficulty discriminating between commercial and program content, and host-selling significantly enhances older children's attitudes toward the product.

94. Laczniak, Gene R., and Patrick E. Murphy. *Marketing Ethics.* Lexington, Massachusetts: Lexington Books, 1985.

    Focuses comprehensively on ethics in advertising, field sales, sales management, price setting, multinational marketing and marketing research. It is designed to help managers control and review their ethical atmosphere. Articles are included that discuss issues of developing foundations for analyzing marketing ethics.

\*   Lewis, E. St. Elmo. *Financial Advertising, for Commercial and Savings Banks, Trust Title Insurance, and Safe Deposit Companies, Investment Houses.* Cited above as item 18.

95. "Inclusion of Social-Responsibility Themes by Magazine Advertisers: A Longitudinal Study." *Journal of Advertising* 15 (2, 1986): 35-41.

    Reports the results of a content analysis of of magazine advertisements appearing during the years 1967, 1972, 1975, 1977, and 1984. Advertisements were classified by whether they included social responsibility themes, by media, and by social responsibility message.

96. Maynard, Joyce. "Into the Mouths of Babes." *SCAN* (condensed from *ADWEEK/Midwest*) August, 1985: 18.

    Describes the effects which television advertising has had on children. Advertising, in addition to promoting products, has molded lifestyles.

97. Moore, Timothy E. "Subliminal Advertising: What You See Is What You Get." *Journal of Marketing* Spring 1928: 38-47.

Evaluates research and arguments in favor of the effectiveness of subliminal advertising techniques on consumer behavior. Finds that while subliminal stimuli have a small effect on affective reactions, the marketing significance of subliminal advertising has yet to be proved.

\* Nichols, Len M. "Advertising and Economic Welfare." Cited above as item 52.

\* Pease, Otis A. "Advertising Ethics." pp 1-5. Cited above as item 23.

98. Quarles, Rebecca Colwell and Lea W. Jeffres. "Advertising and National Consumption: A Path Analytic Re-Examination of the Galbraithian Argument." *Journal of Advertising* 12 (2, 1983): 4-13, 33.

    Re-examines the issue of the relationship between advertising and national consumption. Using data collected on 53 nations, the authors find little evidence that advertising is the major force affecting national consumption. Advertising is found to be a function of consumption, rather than the converse as proposed by Galbraith.

99. Reid, Leonard N., and Lawrence C. Soley. "Generalized and Personalized Attitudes Toward Advertising's Social and Economic Effects." *Journal of Advertising* 11 (3, 1982): 3-7.

    Reports the results of a survey to determine whether differences existed between people's generalized and personalized attitudes toward the social and economic effects of advertising. The survey shows that people are negative toward advertising on the personalized level than the generalized level.

100. Rotzoll, Kim B., James E. Haefner, and Charles H. Sandage. *Advertising in Contemporary Society*. Cincinnati, Ohio: South-Western Publishing Co., 1986.

Discusses contemporary issues in advertising. The authors begin with a discussion of the basic perspectives of advertising and a review of the history of marketing theory. They then discuss current issues, including advertising and economics, advertising audiences, media topics, regulation, and ethics.

101. Scammon, Debra L., and Richard J. Semenik. "The FTC's 'Reasonable Basis' for Substantiation of Advertising: Expanded Standards and Implications." *Journal of Advertising* 12 (1, 1983): 4-11.

    Presents the Federal Trade Commission's theories of deception and its remedies as set forth in the *American Home Products* decision. The implications of standards and corrective advertising for advertisers are discussed.

102. Schulte, Theodore. "Getting to the Underlying Truth on Subliminal Ads." *SCAN* (condensed from *Advertising Age*) May 1985: 5.

    Argues that there is no such thing as planned subliminal advertising and objects to the hype surrounding subliminal advertising.

103. Sheffet, Mary Jane. "An Experimental Investigation of the Documentation of Advertising Claims." *Journal of Advertising* 12 (1, 1983): 19-29.

    Reports the results of an experiment to see whether the disclosure of the existence of product test results would be valued by the subjects. This comes in response to the FTC's Advertising Substantiation Program.

104. Simon, Julian L. *Issues in the Economics of Advertising*. Urbana, Illinois: University of Illinois Press, 1970.

    Examines both the microeconomic and macroeconomic impacts of advertising. The relationships between advertising and product demand, sales and profits are discussed in detail. The economic development of advertising and the effect of advertising on the nation's propensity to consume and social welfare are also discussed.

105. Soley, Lawrence, and Gary Kwizbard. "Sex in Advertising: A Comparison of 1964 and 1984 Magazine Advertisements." *Journal of Advertising* 15 (3, 1986): 46-54, 64.

A content analysis of sexual portrayals in magazine ads during 1964 and 1984. Although the percentage of ads using sexual portrayal did not increase, the sexual portrayals were more overt in 1984 and relied more heavily on visual rather than verbal sex than in 1964. Female models are more likely to be sexually depicted than male models.

106. Stayman, Douglas Mark. *Emotional Response to Advertising: Beyond Attitude Toward the Ad.* Ph. D. Dissertation, University of California, Berkeley, 1985.

Presents the results of four studies of the nature of emotional responses to advertising appeals. The effects of repetition, sequences of commercials and liking the ad on the warmth response are studied.

107. Stein, M. L. "Ad Copy Can Cause Libel Suits, Too," *Editor and Publisher*, October 13, 1984: 18.

Explains how newspapers can be sued for libel arising from advertisements. Ad libel suits can be potentially more damaging to a publisher than editorial suits because the complaining parties are rarely public figures. Offers suggestions for reducing libel risk.

108. Stephens, Nancy and Mary Ann Stutts. "Preschoolers' Ability to Distinguish Between Television Programming and Commercials," *Journal of Advertising* 11 (2, 1982): 16-26.

Proposes a model which predicts children's ability to distinguish between programs and commercials. Supports the proposition that preschoolers respond to perceptual cues and do not recognize the difference between programs and commercials.

109. Taylor, Ronald A. "Billboard Still King of the Road," *U. S. News & World Report.* 10 December 1985: 96.

    Discusses the Highway Beautification Act of 1965 which attempted to limit billboard clutter on freeways. The statute has been amended over the years to favor advertisers, and in many states the act is not enforced, thus defeating its original purpose.

110. Vaile, Roland S. *Economics of Advertising.* New York: Garland Publishing, Inc., 1985. Reprint.

    Considers the economic repercussions of advertising including the issues of cost of manufacturing and consumer education in 1927. The author attempts to determine whether the money spent on advertising is economically and socially justified.

111. "Watch out for the Neo-Prohibitionists," *Marketing and Media Decisions.* February 1984: 48.

    Reports on political action groups which claim that advertising of alcoholic beverages causes people (including young people) to drink too much. The groups seek to restrict such advertising. Raises the issue of whether prohibition of advertising could be the first step to prohibition of sales.

112. "Whopper Ad Budgets: Fast Money for Fast Food," *Business and Society Review.* Fall 1985: 56-60.

    In 1984, over $750 million was spent by fast food chains on advertising, an amount comparable to the amount spent nationwide on child nutrition programs. A group of eight advertising executives and social commentators discuss whether this is a misallocation of resources. Opinions vary, but most see advertising as an important part of free market economics.

113. Wright, John S., and John E. Mertes. *Advertising's Role in Society*. St. Paul: West Publishing Co., 1974.

    A compilation of 63 articles reflecting current (1968-1973) thought on advertising is considered from various points of view, including government, the economy, ethics, consumers, businesses, and society at large.

114. Zanot, Eric J., J. David Pincus, and E. Joseph Lamp. "Public Perceptions of Subliminal Advertising," *Journal of Advertising* 12 (1, 1983): 39-45.

    Reports the results of a survey of current public awareness and attitudes of subliminal advertising. The public, especially the educated, are highly aware of subliminal advertising.

## Motivation and Psychological Issues

115. Adams, Henry Foster. *Advertising and Its Mental Laws.* New York: Garland Publishing, Inc., 1985. Reprint.

    This scientific approach to advertising breaks down the persuasive process into workable definitions. Quantitative techniques as they apply to advertising psychology are analyzed in this rigorous text.

116. Alwitt, Linda F. and Andrew A. Mitchell, editors. *Psychological Processes and Advertising Effects.* Hillsdale, New Jersey: Lawrence Erlbaum Associates, Inc., 1985.

    Thirteen scholarly papers discuss various topics in advertising and consumer psychology. The works are divided into four units dealing with affective reactions to advertising, persuasion processes, the psychological processes of television viewing, and audience involvement with advertisements.

117. Bello, Daniel C., Robert W. Pitts, and Michael I. Etzel. "The Communication Effects of Controversial Sexual Content in Television Programs and Commercials." *Journal of Advertising* 12 (3, 1983): 32-42.

    Examines the effect of controversial sexual content on the communication effectiveness of television advertising messages using interest in the commercial, affect toward product, and purchase intent as measures of communication effectiveness.

118. Caballero, Majorie J., and Paul J. Soloman. "Effects of Model Attractiveness on Sales Response." *Journal of Advertising* 13 (1, 1984): 17-23, 33.

Attempts to determine the effect of the attractiveness and sex of models in point-of-purchase displays on buyer behavior. Three questions are addressed: What is the optimal level of attractiveness? Do responses vary according to the sex of the model and/or the sex of the buyer? Do responses vary according to the type of product being advertised?

119. Craig, C. Samuel, and Brian Sternthal, editors. *Repetition Effects over the Years: An Anthology of Classic Articles.* New York: Garland Publishing, Inc., 1985.

A collection of articles from the psychology literature which discusses how advertisements are remembered and examines how basic psychologial principles relate to advertising.

120. Crosier, Keith. "A New Strategy for Advertising to Over-Communicated Target Audiences," *The Quarterly Review of Marketing*, 7 (July 1982): 13-21.

Focuses on consumer information overload and how the advertiser can avoid the problem by rearranging priorities in the consumers' minds rather than by burdening the audience with too much information.

121. Debevec, Kathleen, and Easwar Iyer. "The Influence of Spokespersons in Altering a Product's Gender Image," *Journal of Advertising* 15 (4, 1986): 12-20.

Investigates whether a spokesperson's gender can influence the gender image of products and finds that the spokesperson's gender is an effective cue in altering the gender image of a masculine or feminine product but not a neutral product.

122. Dichter, Ernest. *The Strategy of Desire.* New York: Garland Publishing, Inc., 1985. Reprint.

123. Durgee, Jeffrey F. "Self Esteem Advertising," *Journal of Advertising*. 15 (1986), no. 4: 21-28.

Describes how consumers' feelings of self-esteem can be leveraged to affect buying behavior. An increasing number of advertisements use self-esteem building as a motivational tool. Durgee suggests that advertisements which have positive effects on consumers' attitudes toward themselves also positively affect consumer attitudes toward the product.

124. Gresham, Larry G., and Terence A. Shimp. "Attitude Toward the Advertisement and Brand Attitudes: A Classical Conditioning Perspective." *Journal of Advertising* 14 (1, 1985): 10-17, 49.

Examines the attitude toward the ad construct in the content of classical conditioning. Concludes that effect generated by television commercials has a direct influence on attitudes toward the advertised brands. Other variables may exist in this relationship.

125. Griffin, George. "Psychographics." *Graphic Arts Monthly*. November 1985: 134-37.

Discusses the use of graphical images in advertising in order to achieve a psychological effect on the potential buyer. The effects could include increased motivation, readership, or memory. One example presented is the bold dotted line around coupons which encourages cutting.

\* Grossbart, Sanford, Darrel D. Muehling, and Norman Kangun. "Verbal and Visual References to Competition in Comparitive Advertising." Cited above as item 47.

126. Heflin, Debbora T. A., and Robert C. Haygood. "Effects of Advertising Messages," *Journal of Advertising* 14 (2, 1985): 41-47, 64.

Examines the effects of scheduling of message exposures on memory of advertisements. Four schedules consisting of one day, one week, three weeks and five weeks are compared, and the one and three week schedules are found to be superior to the others. A model is proposed which explains the differences.

* Hendon, Donald W., and Emelda L. Williams. "Winning the Battle for Your Customer." Cited above as item 51.

127. Hollingworth, Harry Levi. *Advertising and Selling: Principles of Appeal and Response.* New York: Garland Publishing, Inc., 1985. Reprint.

Focuses on the psychological forces which can be used when creating advertisements. Hollingworth discusses catching and holding attention, fixing an impression, and getting a response. Includes analysis of successful and unsuccessful advertisements.

128. Joseph, W. Benoy. "The Credibility of Physically Attractive Communicators: A Review." *Journal of Advertising* 11 (3, 1982): 15-24.

Reviews experimental evidence regarding the effects of physically attractive communicators on recall, persuasion, and product evaluation. Physically attractive communicators are found to have a positive impact upon the products they sell. The authors also review previous studies in this topic.

129. Kilbourne, William E., Scott Painton, and Danny Ridley. "The Effect of Sexual Embedding on Responses to Magazine Advertisements." *Journal of Advertising* 14 (2, 1985): 48-56.

Presents the results of two empirical studies on sexual embedding's effects. One study showed that sexual embedding aided attitudinal evaluations of a liquor ad but not a cigarette ad.

Another study showed that embedding was effective in increasing both advertisements GSR measurements.

\* Kunkel, Dale Lyman. *Children's Understanding of Television Advertising: The Impact of Host-Selling.* Cited above as item 93.

130. Lucas, D. B. and C. E. Benson. *Psychology for Advertisers.* New York: Garland Publishing, Inc., 1985. Reprint.

    Examines the psychological concepts involved in advertising. Included are discussions of media, production and creativity. This 1930 reprint gives examples of magazine advertising.

131. Macklin, M. Carole, and Richard H. Kolbe. "Sex Role Stereotyping in Children's Advertising: Current and Past Trends." *Journal of Advertising* 13 (2, 1984): 34-42.

    Presents the results of a content analysis of 64 television commercials toward children focusing on sex role stereotyping. The study suggests that little change has taken place in the past decade regarding ad dominance, active/passive behavior, aggressive behavior, voice-overs and music.

132. Madden, Thomas J., and Marc G. Weinberger. "The Effects of Humor on Attention in Magazine Advertising," *Journal of Advertising* 11 (3, 1982): 8-14.

    Investigates whether humor in magazine advertisements increased attention to the ads. Utilizing Starch readership scores for humorous liquor ads during the period 1976-1979, humorous ads were shown to outperform nonhumorous ads.

133. Mertes, John E. "The Advertisement as Metacommunication," *Business Perspectives*, Spring 1970: 13-18.

    Discusses the non-verbal communication of advertising. The elements of an advertisement discussed include physical elements such as headline and illustrations, design elements such as size, contrast and harmony, and psychological elements. Psychological elements include the laws of association, repetition, primary, recency, effect and interest. Explains how physical and design elements can elicit the psychological elements.

134. Martineau, Pierre. *Motivation in Advertising: Motives That Make People Buy.* New York: McGraw-Hill Book Company, Inc., 1971.

    Discusses the psychological laws of attention and association and their use in advertising. Advertising is stressed as a dynamic process.

\* Moore, Timothy E. "Subliminal Advertising: What You See Is What You Get." Cited above as item 97.

\* Preston, Ivan L. "The Association Model of the Advertising Communication Process." Cited above as item 58.

\* Scott, Walter Dill. *The Theory of Advertising: A Simple Exposition of the Principles of Psychology in Their Relation to Successful Advertising.* Cited above as item 65.

135. Soldow, Gary F. "The Processing of Information in the Young Consumer: The Impact of Cognitive Developmental Stage on Television, Radio, and Print Advertising." *Journal of Advertising* 12 (3, 1983): 4-14.

    Compares the cognitive responses of children to print, radio, and television advertising focusing on package recall and recognition. Older children showed better recall than younger children; however, young children performed better than expected. Appropriate attentional strategies are discussed.

\* Stayman, Douglas Mark. *Emotional Response to Advertising: Beyond Attitudes Toward the Ad.* Cited above as item 106.

\* Stephens, Nancy, and Mary Ann Stutts. "Preschoolers' Ability to Distinguish Between Television Programming and Commercials." Cited above as item 108.

136. Stout, Patricia Ann. *Emotional Response to Advertising.* Ph.D. dissertation. University of Illinois at Urbana-Champaign, 1985.

    Studies respondents' reactions to 50 television commercials in an effort to identify ads which elicit much emotional response and to discriminate the differences between the ads which elicit response and those which do not.

137. Whipple, Thomas W., and Alice E. Courtney. "Female Role Portrayals in Advertising and Communication Effectiveness: A Review." *Journal of Advertising* 14 (3, 1985): 4-8, 17.

    Reviews and discusses studies concerning model gender—product interactions, female role setting depictions and degree of liberatedness. Evaluates the communication effectiveness of female role portrayals and describes implications for advertising research and practice.

## Reference Guides

The advertising practioner often needs guides for continuous reference. In this and the following two sections reference guides, and a listing of advertising-related periodicals and text books are included.

138. *Advertising Agencies: What They Are, What They Do, and How They Do It.* New York: American Association of Advertising Agencies, Inc., 1976.

    An exposition of the advertising agency's role in the marketing process, this work addresses the prospective advertiser. Topics discussed include advertisement preparation, agency selection, commissions, contracting, and agency organization.

139. *Advertising Compliance Service.* Westport, Connecticut: Greenwood Press, Inc., 1986.

    A comprehensive cumulation of significant developments in advertising regulation for advertisers and their attorneys. A basic reference volume includes pertinent federal, state, industry, and private decisions and legislation which affects advertising. This volume is augmented bi-weekly by the newsletter, *Products and Services Compliance Report.*

140. *Art Index.* New York: The H. W. Wilson Company, 1929-present.

    Published quarterly with a bound cumulation each year, the *Art Index* covers periodicals concerned with the visual arts. Articles are arranged alphabetically by subject. A good source for those concerned with ad production and art direction.

## 42 American Advertising

\* Assael, Henry, and C. Samuel Craig, editors. *The History of Advertising.* New York. Cited above as item 3.

141. *Business Index.* Belmont, California: Information Access Company, 1980-present.

    The most comprehensive index to business sources, the *Business Index* covers over 460 business periodicals and business articles from 1100 general periodicals. Available on computer output microfilm which is read on a special viewer supplied with the subscription. Coverage for each cumulation extends over two or three years. Subjects and names are arranged alphabetically.

142. *Business Periodicals Index.* New York: H. W. Wilson Company, 1958-present.

    Published monthly with a bound cumulation each year, the *Business Periodicals Index* provides a listing of current articles in business and trade magazines. Most major advertising and public relations journals are indexed. Citations are arranged alphabetically.

143. Caples, John. *How To Make Your Advertising Make Money.* Englewood Cliffs, New Jersey: Prentice-Hall, Inc., 1983.

    This "how-to" book contains suggestions for creating and developing advertising ideas. Caples includes extensive guidelines for the various types of writing involved in advertising: copy, sales letters, radio-TV ads, and headlines. Includes case histories, examples, and illustrations.

144. "Glossary of Advertising Media, Marketing, and Promotion Terms." *Supermarketing,* July 1970 (detachable supplement).

    A dictionary of marketing, advertising and promotion terms which are used in all major media attempts to bring the language of Madison Avenue to Main Street. A useful tool for improving communication between advertising agency and client.

145. Gross, Edmund J. *Copy Stimulators.* North Hollywood, California: Halls of Ivy Press, 1975.

Contains 56 categories of headlines and 1,000 advertising words arranged in alphabetical order. This book is intended for use as an idea generator. It is not meant for use as a source of headlines. The example headlines given have been effectively used in advertisements, mailers, etc. This is a great source to stimulate creativity.

146. Hendon, Donald W. *Battling for Profits: How to Win Big on the Marketing Battlefield.* Chattanooga, Tennessee: Business Consultants International, 1986.

Extends the military analogy to marketing management. Chapter thirteen discusses the various areas of the promotional mix including media, sales promotion, public relations, institutional advertising, ad content, the promotion budget, the advertising agency, and personal selling. A good source book for the advertising manager.

147. Hodgson, Richard S. *Direct Mail & Mail Order Handbook*, Second Edition. Chicago: The Dartnell Corporation, 1977.

This comprehensive reference explains the techniques and principles of successful direct mail advertising. Although it stresses that there are no hard and fast rules, the book offers guidelines for increasing effectiveness of a direct mail campaign.

148. Koatz, Ronald B. *Cable: An Advertiser's Guide to the New Electronic Media.* Chicago: Crain Books, 1983.

This book provides practical information for those interested in cable advertising. Message targeting and measurement of results are discussed, and a glossary of new media terms is included.

149. Lichtenberger, John. *Advertising Compliance Law: Handbook for Marketing Professionals and Their Counsel.* Westport, Connecticut: Quorum Books, 1986.

A readable, comprehensive guide to advertising restrictions. Analyzes hundreds of state and federal statutes and regulations; landmark state and federal court decisions; decisions of the FTC, FCC, and NAD/ NARB; and industry self-regulation guidelines. Special types of advertising such as those relating to tobacco, alcohol, professional fields, and politics are examined. A good guide for both laymen and expert.

150. "New World of Advertising." *Advertising Age*, Special issue, 21 November 1973.

This issue gives an indepth summary of the advertising business. The ad agency, media, trade associations, advertising regulations, and marketing research are all discussed here. Also, there is a section dealing with society and advertising and international advertising. A debate is included on the pros and cons of advertising.

151. *1984 Directory for Advertisers.* Second Edition. Norristown, Pennsylvania: Pin Oak, Inc., 1984.

This directory is a guide to where and how to expose advertising to the largest, most interested audience at the lowest cost.

\* Norins, Hanley. *The Complete Copywriter: A Comprehensive Guide to All Phases of Advertising Communication.* Cited as item 256.

152. "100 Leading National Advertising Expenditures by Rank Rank ($000)." *Advertising Age*, September issues.

Each September, the top 100 national advertisers are listed in order of advertising dollars spent nationally. In addition, national advertising spending is grouped by industry, then percent of sales for easy comparison.

153. Paetzel, Hans W., editor. *Complete Multilingual Dictionary of Advertising, Marketing & Communications: English-French-German.* Chicago, Illinois: Crain Books, 1986.

A thorough reference that translates over 8000 technical communications terms in three languages—English, French, and German. A comprehensive guide that is essential for people involved with mass communications.

154. *Reader's Guide to Periodical Literature.* New York: H. W. Wilson Co., 1900-present.

    Presents a broader, general interest approach to coverage of articles in magazines, arranged alphabetically by subject and author. The *Reader's Guide* is not as helpful for serious research as the other indexes, as it excludes many trade and scholarly journals.

155. *SRDS Consumer Magazine and Agri-Media Rates and Data.* 1918. 12. Wilmette, Illinois: Standard Rate and Data Service, Inc.

    A complete guide to buying advertising space in magazines. Magazines are categorized by type (sports, women's, etc.), and each entry contains publications and circulation information and advertising specifications and rates. Published monthly.

156. *SRDS Newspaper Rates and Data.* 1918. 12. Wilmette, Illinois: Standard Rate and Data Service, Inc.

    Lists newspapers in major U.S. markets and gives advertising buying data for each including rates, format, closing times, circulation, and publication information. Published monthly.

157. *SRDS Spot Radio Rates and Data.* 1918. 12. Wilmette, Illinois: Standard Rate and Data Service, Inc.

    A comprehensive guide to spot radio advertising opportunities. Every radio station in major U.S. markets is listed and information is given on station format, network affiliations, agency representatives, and advertising rates. Published monthly. Arranged by state and sub-classified by city.

158. *SRDS Spot Television Rates and Data.* 1918. 12. Wilmette, Illinois: Standard Rate and Data Service, Inc.

Gives comprehensive spot television advertisement buying guide to the stations in major U.S. markets. Information includes station format, network affiliations, advertising rates, and closing times. Published monthly. Arranged by state and sub-classified by city. Published monthly.

159. *Standard Directory of Advertisers.* New York: National Register Publishing Company, 1986.

The "Advertiser Red Book" as it is commonly called is a listing of over 17,000 national and regional firms which are major advertisers. Published annually in two editions, the Classified Edition and Geographical Edition. The Geographical Edition lists advertisers by geographical area, the Classified Edition by product classification. Information on each company includes: name, address, phone number, type of business, management personnel, advertising agency, time and amount of appropriations, and advertising media. A tradename list indexes the companies by product trade names.

160. Stansfield, Richard H. *Advertising Manager's Handbook.* Chicago: The Dartnell Corp., 1979.

This reference focuses almost entirely on industrial advertising. Major portions are devoted to creating copy and layout, while actual management (budgeting, organization, agency relations) is treated more tersely. Contains hundreds of illustrations and case histories. A good encyclopedia-type reference.

161. Urdang, Laurence editor. *Dictionary of Advertising Terms.* Chicago, Illinois: Crain Books, 1983.

This mini-encyclopedia contains functional vocabularies of all segments in the marketing and advertising sphere. More than 4,000 easy-to-understand entries make this a resource essential for both the student and professional.

162. *Wall Street Journal Index.* New York: Dow Jones, 1958-present.

Issued monthly and cumulated annually, this index covers *Wall Street Journal.* Each issue is divided into two parts: Corporate News and General News, and each part is arranged alphabetically by subject heading. A brief abstract is given with each citation.

*Professional Journals and Periodicals*

Each journal entry contains the following:

Journal title. Date of origin. Number of issues per year. Publisher's name and address. A brief description of the journal.

163. *Advertising Age.* 1930. 52. Chicago: Crain Communications.

   A weekly newspaper of happenings and developments in the advertising and public relations profession. Articles and columns in each issue discuss new technologies and techniques, chronicle current advertising campaigns, and report on the actions and conditions of agencies and advertisers. Each September, one issue is devoted to the "100 Leading National Advertising Expenditures by Rank ($000)."

164. *American Demographics.* 1979. 12. Ithaca, New York: American Demographics, Inc.

   A monthly publication concerned with reporting the latest research on demographic trends in America. Oriented toward the marketer, *American Demographics* provides an interesting source of data for target market and audience decisions.

165. *Art Direction.* 1949. 12. New York: Advertising Trade Publications, Inc.

   A lavishly illustrated monthly periodical for the advertising art director. *Art Direction* not only covers the usual technical and technological advances that are featured by trade journals; the journal also includes features about currently used ideas and the current advertisements which make best use of art.

166. *Business Marketing* (formerly *Industrial Marketing*). 1915. 12. Chicago: Crain Communications, Inc.

    A monthly journal concerned with business-to-business marketing. Columns and articles deal with the broader marketing techniques and strategies as well as specific topics in advertising.

167. *Chain Store Age Executive.* 1924. 12. New York: Lebhar-Friedman, Inc.

    A monthly newsmagazine which focuses on retail management. Regular columns feature advertising and promotion of the retail outlet, and occasional articles are devoted to advertising.

168. *Communication Arts.* 1958. 8. Palo Alto, California: Coyne and Blanchard, Inc.

    A highly illustrated magazine which is devoted to the commercial visual arts. Published eight times a year, features includes spreads of prominent commercial artists' work, and innovative advertising. Special issues contain the magazine's choices for best advertisements, photography, and design.

169. *Current Issues and Research in Advertising.* 1978. 1. Ann Arbor, Michigan: Division of Research, School of Business, University of Michigan.

    An annual publication which is a collection of original articles on advertising. The articles are divided into two broad categories: Theory, Practice and Current Developments, and Research. Essentially an academic publication.

170. *Direct Marketing.* 1938. 12. Garden City, New York: Hoke Communications, Inc.

Published monthly, *Direct Marketing* is a trade journal which features articles and columns dealing with selling to both consumer and business markets. In addition to news from the industry, most issues focus on a certain aspect of direct marketing, for example production, telemarketing, and advertising.

171. *Editor & Publisher, The Fourth Estate.* 1901. 52. New York: Editor & Publisher Company.

Published weekly, this journal of the newspaper industry contains a wide variety of articles concerned with newspaper production and management. Weekly columns are concerned with advertising, sales promotion, and production technology as are usual articles.

172. *Graphic Arts Monthly, and the Printing Industry.* 1929. 13. New York: Technical Publishing.

A technical journal for the printing industry. Published monthly plus one special issue each October, *Graphic Arts Monthly* contains articles about developments in printing technology and methods. The special issue is a buyer's guide to printing industry products and suppliers.

173. *Harvard Business Review.* 1922. 6. Boston: Graduate School Business Administration, Harvard University.

A bimonthly journal devoted to the continuing education of professional managers. *HBR* contains articles dealing with any area of business and economics. Frequent articles on advertising and promotion feature a pragmatic, managerial approach.

174. *Imprint.* 1966. 4. Philadelphia, Pennsylvania: Advertising Specialty Information Network.

A quarterly magazine which focuses on specialty advertising ideas. Issues present new creative ideas for using unique channels of promotion.

175. *Industrial Marketing Management.* 1971. 4. New York: Elsevier Science Publishing Company, Inc.

A scholarly journal of industrial marketing published quarterly. Although most articles deal with other aspects of marketing, occasional articles focus on business-to-business advertising.

176. *Inside Print.* 1979. 14. Stanford, Connecticut: M. P. E., Inc.

Published fourteen times a year, *Inside Print* chronicles advertising in magazines. The latest trends in magazine advertising, copy and advertising research, and agency activity are usual topics for articles and columns.

177. *International Advertiser* (Incorporating *Advertising World*). 1973. 6. New York: Directories International, Inc.

Published bimonthly, *International Advertiser* chronicles developments in global advertising. The typical issue is practitioner oriented and contains industry news and articles about all facets of advertising in an international context.

178. *Journal of Advertising.* 1972. 4. Laramie, Wyoming: American Academy of Advertising.

A quarterly journal which focuses on advertising as a communication device and the relationship between communications and the other components of the advertising process. Articles are both theoretical and empirical in nature and are written primarily by and for academics. Includes current book reviews.

179. *Journal of Advertising History.* 1978. 2. Bradford, England: History of Advertising Trust.

Published every six months, this English journal seeks to chronicle the contributions of outstanding campaigns and characters to the field. Articles and book reviews are given on all aspects of advertising.

180. *Journal of Advertising Research.* 1960. 6. New York: Advertising Research Foundation.

   This bimonthly journal presents findings and criticism of advertising research. It is intended primarily for practitioners and users of advertising research.

181. *Journal of Consumer Affairs.* 1966. 2. Columbia, Missouri: American Council on Consumer Interests.

   Published semiannually; features articles and book reviews on issues of consumer interest and consumer protection. Occasional articles discuss consumerism advertising and regulation of advertising.

182. *Journal of Consumer Research.* 1974. 4. Pasadena, California: The Journal of Consumer Research, Inc.

   Published quarterly, this scholarly journal is concerned with reporting findings from research in consumer behavior. Advertising articles deal mainly with the effects of advertising on consumers and consumer learning and information processing.

183. *Journal of Direct Marketing.* 1987. 4. Evanston, Illinois: Medill School of Journalism, Northwestern University.

   A quarterly journal devoted to bridging the gap between direct marketing practitioners and the academic and research community, *JDM* features articles on direct marketing and promotion. Also contains book and software reviews and abstracts of articles of interest in other journals.

184. *Journal of Marketing.* 1936. 4. Chicago: American Marketing Association.

   Published quarterly, this is an academic journal of the broader field of marketing. Often includes articles on advertising and promotion.

185. *Journal of Marketing Research.* 1964. 4. Chicago: American Marketing Association.

Published four times annually, this journal presents quantitative findings of marketing research. Often includes studies of advertising and book reviews.

186. *Journal of Retailing.* 1925. 4. New York: New York University.

Published quarterly, the journal seeks to present new contributions to the theoretical and practical understanding of retail selling. Although there are occasional articles on retail advertising and promotion, most deal with other topics in the broad field of retailing.

187. *Marketing Communications* (Formerly *Printer's Ink*). New York: Media Horizons, Inc.

The oldest periodical concerned with marketing, *Marketing Communications* features current developments in the field of marketing, promotion, and advertising.

188. *Marketing and Media Decisions.* 1965. 12. New York: Decisions Publications Inc.

Published monthly, this journal is edited for those advertising professionals involved in media planning. Columns and articles discuss the latest techniques and developments in all media and the activities of media managers. Itself an advertising forum for the media, *Decisions* is a good source for the media planner.

189. *Marketing News.* 1966. 26. Chicago: American Marketing Association.

A biweekly newspaper of the American Marketing Association. Articles and columns focus on advertising and promotion, market research, marketing management and other marketing-related topics. New techniques and technologies as well as current general industry news are popular topics.

190. *Public Relations Journal*. 1945. 12. New York: Public Relations Society of America.

A professional journal of the public relations field. Articles and columns discuss developments in public relations. Published monthly. Some articles on advertising do appear.

191. *Public Relations Quarterly*. 1956. 4. Rhinebeck, New York: Public Relations Quarterly.

More theoretically oriented than *Public Relations Journal*, *Public Relations Quarterly* features articles by both academics and practitioners. Articles discuss most aspects of PR, including international public relations, new technologies, PR/journalism education, and others.

192. *Public Relations Review*. 1975. 4. Silver Spring, Maryland: Foundation for Public Relations Research and Education, Inc.

Published quarterly, *Public Relations Review* is an academic journal in the PR field. Articles discuss recent contributions to the theoretical base of PR. Especially useful is the winter issue which contains a bibliography of articles and book reviews in public relations published that year.

193. *Sales and Marketing Management* (Formerly *Sales Management*). 1919. 16. New York: Bill Communications, Inc.

A publication concerned with all phases of marketing, *Sales and Marketing Management* is published monthly plus four special issues each year. The special issues: The Survey of Buying Power parts I and II, The Survey of Selling Costs, and The Survey of U.S. Industrial and Commercial Buying Power are most helpful to advertisers. These issues contain tabular data on population, income, sales, selling costs and industries for American markets, data helpful for target market and audience decisions.

194. *SCAN*. 1953. 12. Chicago: The Advertising Checking Bureau.

A *Reader's Digest*-type journal of the advertising industry, this monthly journal contains condensed versions of important articles on selling, advertising, and merchandising. Often includes articles from journals like *Advertising Age*, *ADWEEK*, and *Stores*.

195. *Stores*. 1918. 12. New York: National Retail Merchants Association.

    A monthly magazine for retail executives. *Stores* reports on the latest trends and strategies in retail management. Articles about retail advertising and promotion appear frequently.

196. *Television/Radio Age*. 1952. 26. New York: Television Editorial Corporation.

    Published every two weeks, *Television/Radio Age* focuses on current happenings in the broadcasting field, including production, regulatory, and programming trends. In addition to frequent articles, regular columns feature ideas and developments pertaining to commercials.

## Advertising Texts

The advertising and promotion-related textbooks are too numerous to mention. A subjective approach was used in selecting the listing that follows. There are other good textbooks available but space would not allow inclusion of all of them. The authors of this book have personally used many of those texts.

* Aaker, David A. Editor. *Advertising Management.* Cited above as item 31.

* Aaker, David A. and John G. Myers. *Advertising Management.* Cited above as item 32.

197. Anderson, Robert L., and Thomas E. Barry. *Advertising Management: Text & Cases.* Columbus, Ohio: Charles E. Merrill Publishing Company, 1979.

    This text is intended for junior-senior level courses in advertising management. Discusses the advertising department and agency and provides cases, several of which involve actual companies.

198. Barban, Arnold M., Steven M. Cristol, and Frank J. Kopec. *Essentials of Media Planning: A Marketing Viewpoint.* Chicago: Crain Books, 1986.

    Explains how the marketing plan fits into the marketing mix. The basics of media and the importance of strategy and objectives to the planning process are discussed.

199. Bogart, Leo. *Strategy in Advertising.* Second Edition. Chicago: Crain Books, 1986.

This text focuses on creating the most efficient advertising and how to make use of all the options available. The author covers strategy in advertising as well as mass communication and mass media in depth.

200. Bolen, William H. *Advertising*. New York: John Wiley and Sons, Inc., 1986.

This text provides extensive treatment of all major media and production processes including copywriting and production. Cases and illustrations are provided.

201. Book, Albert C., and C. Dennis Schick. *Fundamentals of Copy and Layout*. Chicago: Crain Books, 1984.

This workbook includes assignments for practicing copy, headline, and layout skills in an advertising problem solving context. Presents the creative philosophies of famous names in advertising such as Ogilvy and Bernbach. Six cases are included to further hone advertising skills.

202. Bovie, Courtland L., and William F. Arens. *Contemporary Advertising*, Second Edition. Homewood, Illinois: Irwin, 1986.

A comprehensive introductory advertising textbook. All major aspects of advertising are well covered, especially the media and the role of advertising in the marketing mix. Well illustrated.

203. Burton, Phillip Ward. *Advertising Copywriting*, Third Edition. Columbus, Ohio: Grid, Inc., 1974.

This text is a comprehensive guide to copywriting for all media at levels ranging from national to local. Although its discussion of modern market segmentation and segmentation's effects on copywriting is weak, the book provides a sound reference to most other aspects of copywriting. Examples from well-known campaigns are provided.

204. Burton, Phillip Ward, and Scott C. Purvis, Editors. *Which Ad Pulled Best?* Fifth Edition. Chicago: Crain Books, 1986.

A workbook containing 50 pairs of actual advertisements which illustrate the principles of layout and copywriting which the book discusses.

205. Burton, Phillip Ward, and William Ryan. *Advertising Fundamentals*, Third Edition. Columbus, Ohio: Grid Publishing, Inc., 1980.

This text gives extensive coverage to copywriting for the different media and the advertising department and agency.

\* Calkins, Earnest Elmo, and Ralph Holden, *Modern Advertising*. Cited above as item 4.

\* Cohen, Dorothy. *Advertising*. Cited above as item 5.

206. Crawford, John W. *Advertising*, Second Edition. Boston, Massachusetts: Allyn and Bacon, Inc., 1965.

Focuses on the role and responsibilities of advertising in society. The author discusses the justification of advertising from the viewpoints of society and business, the role of advertising in the marketing program, creativity in advertising, the media, research as the basis for creative decisions and evaluation, and the management of advertising.

207. DeLozier, M. Wayne. *The Marketing Communications Process*. New York: McGraw-Hill, Inc., 1976.

Explores communications principles and how they can be used to enhance the firm's advertising process.

208. Dunn, S. Watson, and Arnold M. Barban. *Advertising: Its Role in Modern Marketing*. Sixth Edition. Chicago: The Dryden Press, 1986.

Provides a bird's eye view of the field of advertising, focusing on the origin and evaluation of advertising, advertising organizations, campaign planning, production, and media.

\* Dyer, Gilliam. *Advertising as Communication.* Cited above as item 6.

\* Engel, James F., Martin R. Warshaw, and Thomas C. Kinnear. *Promotional Strategy*, Sixth Edition. Cited above as item 42.

209. Hall S. Roland. *The Advertising Handbook.* New York: Garland Publishing, Inc., 1985. Reprint.

Detailed description of each step in the advertising planning process is given. This text provides a comprehensive overview of the entire process and compares the strengths and weaknesses of the various media. Illustrations and examples are included.

\* Johson, J. Douglas. *Advertising Today.* Cited above as item 14.

210. Heighton, Elizabeth J., and Don R. Cunningham. *Advertising in the Broadcast Media.* Belmont, California: Wadsworth Publishing Company, Inc., 1976.

This text is divided into four sections: 1. the history of broadcast advertising, 2. developing broadcast campaigns, 3. buying and selling time, and 4. social responsibility. These four sections are designed to cover a broad spectrum yet give some in-depth details of the industry.

211. Katzenstein, Herbert, and William S. Sachs. *Direct Marketing.* Columbus, Ohio: Merrill Publishing Company, 1986.

A comprehensive guide to direct marketing and includes chapters on budgeting, segmenting, direct mail, creating advertising, catalogs and more.

212. Kaufman, Louis C. *Essentials of Advertising*, Second Edition. San Diego, California: Harcourt Brace Jovanovich, 1987.

Takes a pragmatic approach to the field of advertising. The text is divided into five parts: survey of advertising, decisions in advertising, guide to media, creative aspects, and the worlds of advertising. Each of twenty-two chapters concludes with a profile of a prominent individual in advertising and a short case.

213. Kleppner, Otto, Thomas Russell, and Glenn Verrill. *Advertising Procedure*, Eighth Edition. Englewood Cliffs, New Jersey: Prentice-Hall, Inc., 1983.

    Provides the student with a pragmatic guide to advertising practice and the philosophy of advertising as a persuasive communications tool.

214. Mandell, Maurice I. *Advertising*. Englewood Cliffs, New Jersey: Prentice-Hall, Inc., 1968.

    This text presents a comprehensive overview of the profession as seen by a former advertising executive. Especially good is the section on creativity. The sections on advertising management, however, are weak and avoid controversial issues. A good book for the advertising career novice.

215. McCarthy, E. Jerome, and William D. Perreault, Jr. *Basic Marketing: A Managerial Approach*, Eighth Edition. Homewood, Illinois: Richard D. Irwin, Inc., 1984.

    Emphasizes marketing strategy planning. The student gets a look at marketing from the marketing management point of view. This text provides great flexibility and includes behavioral objectives at the beginning of each chapter. Photographs, figures, graphs and a glossary of terms are included as well. A section on advertising is included.

216. Moore, H. Frazier. *Public Relations: Principles, Cases, and Problems*, Eighth Edition. Homewood, Illinois: Richard D. Irwin, Inc., 1984.

62  American Advertising

A basic text in public relations which combines theory and practice. Units discuss the function, tools, audiences, special applications and social responsibility of public relations.

217. Norris, James S. *Advertising*, Third Edition. Reston, Virginia: Reston Publishing Company, Inc., 1984.

A "how-to" book which gives a broad survey of how advertising works at both the national and local levels.

\*    Nylen, David W. *Advertising: Planning, Implementation, and Control*, Third Edition. Cited above as item 53.

218. Quelch, John A., and Paul W. Farris. *Cases In Advertising and Promotion Management*. Homewood, Illinois: Business Publications, Inc., 1986.

This text contains thirty-five classroom tested studies that examine the development and utilization of promotion outlines from the advertiser's point of view. These cases involve situations dealing with industrial, nonprofit, service, and consumer quads. It is accompanied by a teacher's manual and videotape of commercials.

219. Ray, Michael L. *Advertising and Communications Management*. Englewood Cliffs, New Jersey: Prentice-Hall Inc., 1982.

A promotion strategy textbook which emphasizes the communication function of the promotion mix. The usual advertising management topics are discussed, including planning, budgeting, goal setting, organization, the promotional message, the media mix, and evaluation. Not many illustrations of actual ads.

\*    Rossiter, John R., and Larry Percy. *Advertising and Management*. Cited above as item 61.

\*    Rotzoll, Kim B., et al. *Advertising in Contemporary Society*, 1986. Cited above as item 62.

220. Schultz, Don E. *Essentials of Advertising Strategy*. Chicago: Crain Books, 1986.

Deals with the importance and characteristics of a good strategy. The author takes a look at buyer behavior and the buying process. Advertising regulation is discussed as is the difference between advertising and marketing. Advertising is focused on from development to execution with illustration and examples.

221. Simon, Raymond. *Publicity and PR Worktext*, Fourth Edition. Columbus, Ohio: Grid, Inc., 1978.

A worktext designed to teach step by step the elements of public relations. Each unit begins with text which explains concepts to be used in related cases, projects, and assignments.

222. Sissors, Jack Z., and William B. Goodrich. *Media Planning Workbook: With Discussions and Problems*, Second Edition. Chicago: Crain Books, 1983.

A workbook that includes the primary objectives of media planning. This workbook accompanies *Advertising Media Planning*. Assignments are designed to aid in the exercise of primary principles of media problems at the beginning and advanced levels. Tables and exhibits are included.

223. Sissors, Jack Z., and Jim Surmanek. *Advertising Media Planning*, Second Edition. Chicago: Crain Books, 1983.

A text that shows the student how the different media choices fit into the complete marketing strategy. Media planning experts share ideas about choosing and evaluating the types of media. Starting with an introduction to media planning, it also includes selecting the media, putting it together and finally evaluating the choice.

224. Tipper, Harry, George Burton Hotchkiss, Harry L. Hollingworth, and Frank Alvah Parsons. *Advertising, Its Principles and Practices*. New York: Garland Publishing Inc., 1985. Reprint.

Examines various disciplines which are involved in advertising, including economics, psychology, aesthetics and written composition. Within the framework of the advertising campaign, the authors discuss in this 1915 book the economic and psychological factors involved in advertising, copy, media, the ad manager, outdoor advertising and advertising planning.

225. Ulanoff, Stanley M. *Advertising in America.* New York: Hastings House Publishers, 1977.

This introductory advertising text gives a comprehensive review of the field. Advertising management is especially well covered, including discussions of the advertising agency, computer, and auditing groups.

226. Whetmore, Edward Jay. *Mediamerica: Form, Content, and Consequence of Mass Communication,* Third Edition. Belmont, California: Wadsworth Publishing, 1987.

This mass communications textbook devotes a chapter to advertising and public relations in the mass media. The chapter is an overview of mass media advertising and discusses the history of advertising, subliminal advertising, and advertising ethics.

227. Wright, John. S., Daniel S. Warner, Willis L. Winter, Jr., and Sherilyn K. Zeigler. *Advertising*, Fourth Edition. New York: McGraw-Hill, Inc., 1977.

Introductory text to both the creative and managerial sides of advertising. The role of advertising, the media, production, and the advertising campaign are discussed.

\* Wright, John W. *The Commercial Connective—Advertising and the American Mass Media.* Cited above as item 30.

\* Zacher, Robert V. *Advertising Techniques and Management.* Cited above as item 69.

228. Zeigler, Sherilyn K., and Herbert H. Howard. *Broadcast Advertising*. Columbus, Ohio: Grid, Inc., 1978.

Provides a good foundation for students in broadcast advertising. It covers regulations to social responsibility and production to copy testing. The sixteen chapters are good preparation for students in the electronic advertising world.

# CHAPTER TWO

# THE INSTITUTION OF ADVERTISING

# THE INSTITUTION OF ADVERTISING

## Advertising Agencies

Articles and books in this section include agency management, creative/account relationship, agency/client relationship, agency operations, and agency careers. Specific advertising agencies and how to select an agency topics are also included.

229. Adams, Charles F. *Common Sense In Advertising.* New York: McGraw-Hill Book Company, 1965.

    This book discusses the necessity of advertising people to use common sense in regard to creativity. Examines the "seven deadly sins" of advertising: not doing one's homework, talking in ad jargon, relying on the formula, mistaking strangeness for creativity, relying on new cliches, substituting techniques for ideas, and giving in to occupational isolation.

\*   Advertising Agencies: *What They Are, What They Do and How They Do It.* Cited above as item 138.

230. Barton, Roger. *Advertising Agency Operations and Management.* New York: McGraw-Hill Book Company, Inc., 1955.

    This book focuses on how different functions (copy, media, research, public relations, mechanical production, etc.) are organized in an ad agency rather than the roles of the functions.

231. Beltramini, Richard F. "The Impact of Infomercials: Perspectives of Advertisers and Advertising Agencies." *Journal of Advertising Research*, 23 (August/September 1983): 25-31.

This article describes the trend toward "infomercials" and presents the results of a survey of advertisers regarding their use.

232. Brower, Charlie. "My Life, Loves, and Lumps in the Agency Business." *Advertising Age*, 3 May 1971: 39-42.

Charlie Brower writes about his experiences and discusses openly the infighting within BBDO. One of the most interesting sections focuses on the Eisenhower and Nixon presidential campaigns.

233. Buxton, Ed. "Narrowing Down the Field." *SCAN* (condensed from *ADWEEK/Midwest*) August, 1985: 15.

Buxton discusses the high attrition rate of employees of advertising agencies. The business is seen as a young people's business, and few older people remain.

234. Cagley, James W., and C. Richard Roberts. "Criteria for Advertising Agency Selection: An Objective Appraisal." *Journal of Advertising Research* April/ May 1984: 27-31.

Presents the findings of a study which indicate the importance of the "people factor" as a variable used by firms to select and evaluate their advertising agencies.

\* Calkings, Earnest Elma, and Ralph Holden. *Modern Advertising*. Cited above as item 4.

235. Corbin, Frank. "Ad Agency-PR Company Marriages." *SCAN* (condensed from *Madison Avenue*) August, 1986: 1-3.

Discusses the problems and advantages encountered by advertising agencies which incorporated public relations into their activities.

236. Cummings, Bart. *Advertising's Benevolent Dictators.* Chicago: Crain Books, 1986.

Interviews with 18 leading advertising executives reveal how they "ran" their agencies. Those interviewed include Ogilvy and Mather, Leo Burnett, Troate and others.

237. Cummings, Bart A. "Full Service Agencies vs. a La Carte." *Journal of Advertising* Vol. 2 No. 1, 1973: 12-15.

Compares "a la carte" advertising, where the advertiser acts as coordinator of the services of independents with the full service advertising agency and concludes that full-service agencies work for most advertisers.

238. "Dentsu Advertising, Ltd." *The Oriental Economist*, October 1976: 34-36.

The world's largest advertising agency is the topic of this report. This agency controls one fourth of the advertising in Japan and has twenty-two subsidiaries. The agency has expanded into public relations and sales promotion. Financial data on Dentsu are given and compared to two other agencies.

239. Frazer, Charles F. "Creative Strategy: A Management Perspective." *Journal of Advertising* 12 (4, 1983): 36-41.

Suggests that the topic of creative strategy has been given little attention by the advertising management literature and that the identification of strategic alternatives will simplify planning. Seven distinct strategic options are outlined and the characteristics of each are explained.

\* Gardner, Burleigh B. *A Conceptual Framework for Advertising.* Cited above as item 44.

240. Gardner, Herbert S. *The Advertising Agency Business.* Chicago, Illinois: Crain Books, 1983.

A comprehensive publication on the advertising agency business. It contains information on what an agency is worth, how to get started, and what it takes to be a success.

241. Glucroft, Helene. "Theft at Your Expense." SCAN (reprinted from *Advertising Age*) September 1985: 14-16.

    Suggests ways in which internal control can be used by ad agencies to cut down employee misstatement of expenses for travel and entertainment.

242. Haase, Albert E. *The Advertising Appropriation, How To Determine It and How To Administer It.* New York: Garland Publishing, Inc., 1985. Reprint.

    In this 1931 book, Haase discusses advertising, evaluation, and administration. Included are discussions of how to determine advertising appropriation and advertising effectiveness, and how to select and advertising agency.

243. Hotz, Mark K. John K. Ryans, and William K. Skanklin. "Agency/Client Relationships as Seen by Influentials on Both Sides." *Journal of Advertising* 11 (1, 1982): 37-44.

    Reports the results of a survey of agency leaders and leading advertisers to see how agencies and clients feel about each other and the agency/client relationship. Perceptions of the relationship are mostly positive. Suggestions are made for better working relationships based on the findings.

244. Jordan, J. J. "Accountability in Media?" *SCAN* (condensed from *Advertising Age*) May, 1985: 13-15.

    A satirical discussion of media-agency relations that touches several important points, written in response to the elimination of television station logging requirement.

245. Kalish, David. "Keeping Creatives Happy and Creative." *SCAN* (condensed from *ADWEEK*) March 1987: 11-13.

Reports on the advertising agency problem of motivating and managing creative personnel. Kalish offers several suggestions, including keeping loose but present controls, avoiding competition and matching rewards to individual employee desires.

246. Keeler, Floyd Y., and Albert E. Haase. *The Advertising Agency, Procedure and Practice.* New York: Garland Publishing Inc., 1985. Reprint.

    This 1927 book provides insights into the basics of starting and running an advertising agency. Includes suggestions for organization, management and procedures.

247. Kent, Deborah. "When to Fire Your Ad Agency and How to Avoid Needing to." *Business Marketing.* September 1985: 54-56.

    Focuses on ways to maintain and improve agent/ client relations. Factors which destroy relations, including personnel turnover and lack of enthusiasm, are discussed in addition to agency performance evaluation techniques.

248. MacDougall, Malcolm. "The Myths of Bigness." *SCAN* (condensed from *Adweek/Midwest*) July 1986: 1.

    Exposes five myths in promoting the direct relationship between advertising agency size, efficiency, and effectiveness. Concludes that agencies should strive to be the best, not the biggest.

249. Mackie, Valerie, et al. "Advertising: Join it and See the World." *SCAN* (condensed from *Advertising Age*) September 1985: 9-12.

    Shows results of an *Advertising Age* survey of job opportunities with advertising agencies in foreign countries including New Zealand, Australia, Japan, Korea, Britain, Germany, France, The Netherlands, Brazil and South Africa.

250. Mandose, Joe. "Putting a Price on Service." *SCAN* (condensed from *ADWEEK*) May, 1985: 20.

Compensation of an advertising agency is becoming more and more a negotiated process. Spokespersons from agencies such as Ogilvy and Mather, Doyle Dane Bernbach and the Interpublic Group discuss the latest trends in compensation.

251. Marsteller, William A. *Creative Management.* Chicago: Crain Books, 1987.

The management of a creative team, often a very difficult task, is the topic of this work. How to successfully inspire a creative staff to do its best work with enthusiasm.

252. Marsteller, William A. "Marsteller: Do-It-Yourself Is a Costly Agency Substitute." *Industrial Marketing.* May 1971: 54.

Examines the economic and qualitative issues involved in setting up a house agency and concludes that achieving quality with a house agency is beyond the means of most firms because of high overhead costs.

253. Michell, Paul C. N. "Auditing of Agency-Client Relations." *Journal of Advertising Research* December 1986/January 1987: 29-41.

Reports the results of a study on why United States advertisers switch advertising agencies. These results are compared with a parallel study for the United Kingdom.

254. Milsap, Cynthia R. "Ad Agencies Seek Alternate Billing Method." *Business Marketing.* October 1985: 48.

Discusses the progression from commission to flat fee and time-based billing by advertising agencies. Flat fees and time-based billing match revenues with costs better than commissions because they are based on actual agency costs.

255. Morgan, Eric A. *Choosing and Using Advertising Agencies.* London: Business Books, 1974.

Offers the fundamental ideas and insights on how to improve the client-agency relationship. It is designed to help advertisers find a reliable agency, get the most out of their advertising dollar and to show the client how to benefit from this advertising. It also gives information on how to end a relationship with an agency.

256. Moskin, J. Robert. *The Case for Advertising.* New York: American Association of Advertising Agencies, 1973.

An insider's look at the workings of the $20 billion advertising industry and how the advertising industry sells the products of the American economy and communicates through the mass media.

257. Norins, Hanley. *The Compleat Copywriter: A Comprehensive Guide to All Phases of Advertising Communication.* New York: McGraw-Hill Book Company, 1966.

Norins discusses, in a case and example fashion, the advertising copywriter. Although not a technical mannual of copywriting, much insight to the profession is given. The book is divided into three parts: The Message, The Media, and The Future Campaign.

258. Norris, Vincent P. "Toward a Social Control in the Advertising Agency." *Journal of Advertising* 12 (1, 1983): 30-33.

Discusses the extent to which advertising agencies exert social control over their members. The author contends that this often-overlooked aspect of the agency needs to be included in collegiate study.

259. Ogilvy, David. *Confessions of an Advertising Man.* New York: Athenuem, 1980.

Draws on personal experiences as chairman of Ogilvy and Mather to illustrate various principles of advertising. Most chapters are "How to" chapters which focus on running an ad agency, producing advertisements, and having a successful career in advertising. Somewhat autobiographical, with many personal overdates.

76  American Advertising

260. Paskowski, Marianne. "Shades of Grey." *Marketing and Media Decisions*. March 1986: 30.

Focuses on black advertising agencies and the increasing marketing orientation toward blacks. The black population is growing faster than the general population, and advertisers have taken notice.

261. Pattis, S. William. *Advertising Careers*. Chicago: Crain Books, 1986.

Discusses advertising agency operations and careers in advertising. Good overview of the scope of the industry and media relations to advertisers, consumers, and products.

262. Peterson, R. D. "The Evolution of Advertising Agency Services." *Akron Business and Economic Review*, 10 (Summer 1979): 17-23.

Divides the development of advertising agency services into seven stages beginning with inception (1704-1840) and ending with expansion of service (1926-present). Background work, art work, copy, mechanical reproduction and media selection, are essential to placing, planning, and preparing advertising.

263. "Recruiting an Ad Agency." *Mainly Marketing*. September 1971: 1-4.

Offers suggestions for evaluating and choosing an advertising agency, including defining agency responsibilities and exploring the capabilities of the agency. Two "knock out factors" are given: the existence of a Plans Board and whether the agency tries to bypass the ad manager and deal with the head executives.

264. Rosenberg, Merri. "Franchising an Ad Agency." *Venture*. May 1985: 158.

Deals with the franchising activities of AD Net USA, a Massachusetts based agency which deals with small local clients.

The local franchise buys creative and production work from AD Net and sells in the local market.

265. Vanden Bergh, Bruce G., Sandra J. Smith, and Jon L. Wicko. "Internal Agency Relationships: Account Services and Creative Personnel." *Journal of Advertising* 15 (2, 1986): 55-60.

Examines areas of conflict in working relationships between account and creative personnel in advertising agencies. Creative people were found to be more critical of account people than account people were of creative people. Various reasons for these results are explained.

266. Wackman, Daniel B., Charles T. Salmon, and Caryn C. Salmon. "Developing an Advertising Agency-Client Relationship." *Journal of Advertising Research*, December 1986/January 1987: 21-28.

Examines the elements of the agency-client relationship from development to disintegration and identifies the factors which lead to satisfaction at different stages of the relationship.

267. Weilbacher, William M. *Auditing Productivity: Advertiser-Agency Relationships Can Be Improved.* Chicago: Crain Books, 1983.

Shows agencies as well as advertisers how to enhance efficiency of advertising by developing a better working relationship between the two. It evolved from the ANA's Agency Relations Committee research on methods to increase productivity of advertising.

268. Weilbacher, William M. *Choosing an Advertising Agency.* Chicago: Crain Books, 1983.

This trade book takes the client through the process of selecting an advertising agency. It covers every facet of the relationship between the client and the agency. Prior knowledge is not necessary for this book to be useful. Professional advertising people may find little new in this publication.

269. Weinstein, Arnold K. "The International Expansion of U.S. Multinational Advertising Agencies." *Business Topics*. Summer 1974: 29-35.

Considers the entry motivations, entry strategies, and ownership strategies of U.S. advertising agencies which are expanding abroad. Motivated by offensive oppportunities, defensive reactions, client service requirements or the driving force of a senior executive, U.S. firms usually wholly own their foreign subsidiaries and prefer to buy existing agencies.

270. Wolfe, Richard A. "Youth Should, Too, Be Heard in the Ad Business." *Advertising Age*. 29 June 1970: 45.

The author argues that creative departments need youthful talent, citing a lack of young people in advertising copy and art position.

271. "World's Top 50 Ad Agency Groups in 1985." *SCAN* (reprinted from *Advertising Age*) June 1985: 15-16.

Top fifty agency groups in 1985 are listed based on gross income. Total billings and rank in 1984 are included.

272. Wright, John S., and John E. Tully. "The Advertising-Marketing Marriage." *Journal of Advertising*. Vol. 3 No. 2, 1974: 28-33.

Discusses the relationship between advertising agency and marketing using the analogy of marriage. The attributes of an open marriage are compared to the characteristics for a progressive partnership between advertising and marketing. The theory is that good campaigns are a reflection of an open marriage rather than a closed one.

\* Wright, John W. *The Commercial Connection —Advertising and the American Mass Media*. Cited as item 30.

273. Young, James Webb, and J. Walter Thompson. *How To Become an Advertising Man*. Chicago, Illinois: Crain Books, 1986.

This 96 page book contains 50 years or more of Young's achievements. What was once used as a text by Young later became utilized by J. Walter Thompson as a foundation for a training program within the agency.

274. Zetner, Herbert. "1986: A Challenging Year for Advertising." *SCAN* (condensed from *Advertising Age*) February 1986: 1-3.

    Discusses expected spending trends for advertising and promotion for 1986. Budget increases are slowing down, and advertising agencies will struggle to keep up with the change.

275. Zeigenhagen, M. E. "In-House or Outside Agency? Advertisers Must Answer the Key Questions." *Business Marketing.* January 1986: 94.

    Addresses the question of in-house advertising and formulates three conditions which managers should consider when considering in-house advertising. First, the firm must have personnel who can carry out a complete marketing communications program. Second, the company must work out a planning process for marketing the product. Third, this must all be done on a cost-effective basis.

## Suppliers

The people and organizations that specialize in some ancillary aspect of the advertising business are commonly referred to as suppliers. Many of the suppliers are freelance professionals who are selling their respective services. This includes art studios, typesetters, printers and related specialists, film and video production houses and research companies.

276. Alter, Stewart. "Ad Trainees Hit the Trenches." *Advertising Age* October 10, 1985: 2.

    Discusses copywriter recruiting and training efforts by J. Walter Thompson Company and Dancer Fitzgerald Sample. New talent is recruited from other agencies as well as from non-advertising fields.

277. Bailey, Harvey. "What Happened to Copy?" *Advertising Age* October 17, 1985: 67.

    Addresses the question of whether copywriting has taken a back seat to art in advertising. The author agrees that visuals in advertising are increasing in importance and cites the economy, MTV, better art direction, and a better understanding of consumer persuasion as reasons.

278. Blonsky, Marshall. "Photographs Focus on the Image." *Advertising Age* April 4, 1985: 18.

    Discusses several fashion photographers' creative techniques for achieving desired effects. The best photographs, according to the article, always deliver the same impressions in their work.

279. Christensen, Eric. "All About Freelancing." *Editor and Publisher* August 18, 1984: 56, 43.

Discusses freelance copywriting for advertising agencies, including such aspects as how to get started, writer-agency relations, and financial topics.

280. "Communication Arts 1985 Advertising Annual." *Communication Arts* December 1985.

This issue contains 165 pages of advertisements which ran in 1985 and were considered to be among the best work of commercial artists, copywriters and art directors. The media featured include consumer and trade journals, newspaper, broadcast media, outdoor, P.O.P., sales promotion and self-promotion. Production credits are given for each ad.

281. "Communication Arts 1985 Photography Annual." *Communication Arts* August 1985.

Reviews the best commercial photography of 1985, containing 129 pages of color illustrations. Photos are from advertisements, books, editorials, institutional promotions and self-promotion. Each exhibit is briefly identified and explained.

282. Kalish, David. "All the Print That's Fit for News." *Art Direction* January 1985: 53-62.

Reports on the development in recent years of the newspaper as a medium. Technological advances and art director's imagination have led to revival in newspaper advertising, a medium once frowned upon because of poor reproduction. Many illustrations.

283. Kalish, David. "Baby Talk." *Art Direction* April 1985: 84-91.

Discusses the problems faced and techniques used by advertising art directors in casting babies in advertisements. The author likens working with babies to working with animals in that both are unpredictable and must be trained to perform. Illustrated.

284. Lewis, Herschell Gordon. *How To Make Your Advertising Twice as Effective at Half the Cost.* Englewood Cliffs, New Jersey: Prentice-Hall, Inc., 1986.

Covers various aspects of advertising, focusing on effectiveness and economy. Included are print, direct mail and television production techniques, techniques for buying copy and art, and ways to obtain lower-than- cord rates.

285. Mach, Tom. "Would You Make a Top Copywriter?" *Advertising Age* October 8, 1984: 20-22.

Presents a short, humorous quiz which acquaints the reader with some of the principles and difficulties of the advertisement copywriting profession. For example, pleasing the consumer versus the creative director or coping with rejection.

* Pattis, S. William. *Advertising Careers.* Cited above as item 260.

286. Stiansen, Sarah. "Creatives Stay in Advertising for the Money, People." *SCAN* (condensed from *ADWEEK*) December 1986: 6-7.

Reports the results of a survey of creative staffs' attitudes toward their jobs. Creative people are generally less satisfied with their jobs than other agency people and are less ambitious. Creatives prefer to work alone and choose advertising careers because of the money.

287. "That Touch of...Class." *Art Direction* April 1984: 77-83.

Presents twelve print advertisements which, from and art director's perspective, are outstanding examples of craftsmanship. Each illustration is critiqued and includes production credits.

*Media*

Each of the major media available to the advertiser has unique capabilities and unique audience characteristics. The advertiser must plan which media to use to convey the message to the target audience. Then the media planner must select the media class or choice of media use. The media function involves two basic processes of media planning and media selection.

*Media Planning and Selection*

The first part of this section includes media selection models, media/market matching, and advertising measurement. Then the following sections include articles and books from the print media, electronic media, direct marketing media, out-of-home media, sales promotion, and other supplementary media.

288. *Advertising Doesn't Cost...and Other Lies.* Miami, Florida: L. S. Enterprises, 1976.

   Discusses the importance of advertising planning. Media selection is discussed as are the strengths of the various media.

\*   Barban, Arnold M., Steven M. Cristol, and Frank J. Koper. *Essentials of Media Planning: A Marketing Viewpoint.* Cited above as item 198.

289. Barnes, Jimmy D., Brenda J. Moscove, and Javad Rassouli. "An Objective and Task Media Selection Decision Model and Advertising Cost Formula to Determine International

Advertising Budgets." *Journal of Advertising*, 11 (no. 4, 1982): 68-75.

Presents flow charts of objective and task decisions concerning markets media and costs in an international setting. A vital part of the model is a formula for estimating advertising costs which incorporates seven variables.

290. Barton, Roger. *Media in Advertising*. New York: McGraw-Hill Book Company, 1964.

    A comprehensive guide to media planning which contains and provides a basic understanding of the tenets and techniques involved in media mixing.

291. Betancourt, Hal. *The Advertising Answerbook*. Englewood Cliffs, New Jersey: Prentice-Hall, Inc., 1982.

    A guide to professional people which discusses the law and advertising, the planning of budgets, the selection and use of media and the management of advertising professionals.

292. "Big Plans for Media Planning." *SCAN* (reprinted from *Marketing and Media Decisions*) October, 1985: 8-9.

    Discusses the results of a survey of advertising executives' opinions concerning various topics in media planning.

\*   Bogart, Leo. *Strategy in Advertising*, Second Edition. Cited above as item 199.

293. Bush, Alan J., and James H. Leigh. "Advertising on Cable Versus Traditional Networks." *Journal of Advertising Research* April/May 1984: 33-38.

    Reports the results of research concerning content differences between commercials on network and cable television. Cable is found to offer a less cluttered exposure environment than network television, yet in most other respects the uses of commercials were similar.

294. Cannon, Hugh M. "Evaluating the Profile-Distance Approach to Media Selection." *Journal of Advertising* 14 (1, 1985): 4-9.

    Discusses indirect media-target market matching and evaluates the Sissors profile-distance approach. The Sissors approach is found to be valid, but its value relative to other approaches is suspect.

295. Cannon, Hugh M. "Media-Market Matching versus 'Random Walk' in Television Media Selection." *Journal of Advertising Research* April/May 1986: 37-41.

    Compares target market exposure of television advertisements when they are randomly distributed with their exposure where they are matched with programs watched by a given target market. The indirect and direct methods of matching are compared with the random walk, and Cannon finds that both matching methods produce better exposure than the random walk.

296. Cannon, Hugh M. "A Method for Estimating Target Market Ratings in Television Media Selection." *Journal of Advertising* 15 (2, 1986): 21-26.

    Explains how selectivity indexes derived from national product-media data can be combined with data from more specialized television-usage data services to yield an estimate of target market ratings. This method can overcome the shortcomings of nationally syndicated data services.

297. Cannon, Hugh M. "The 'Naive' Approach to Demographic Media Selection." *Journal of Advertising Research* January/June 1984: 21-25.

    Addresses the validity of naive-demographic- indirect matching, a simple media selection approach used by many media planners. Positive and negative attributes are discovered and explained.

298. Chandon, Jean-Louis. *A Comparative Study of Media Exposure Models.* New York: Garland Publishing, Inc., 1985.

Examines and evaluates forty-seven media exposure models with regard to proper audience measurement, relative merits of current methodologies and the discrepancies between the competitive research services for the various media.

299. Clayton, Edward R. and Lawrence J. Moore. "An Interactive Model for Advertising Media Selection." *The Southern Journal of Business*, November 1972: 37-45.

An analysis of the different mixes of media selection through the use of goal programming. Common linear programming specifies a solitary objective while goal programming can handle many demands on scarce resources. This article also examines how the goals can be arranged in order of importance.

300. Cook, Harvey R. *Selecting Advertising Media: A Guide For Small Business.* Washington, D.C.: U.S. Government Printing Office, 1969.

A guide for small businesses to use in selecting media for their specific companies. This guide is a useful tool for all small businesses.

301. Craig, C. Samuel and Avijit Ghosh, editors. *The Development of Media Models in Advertising: An Anthology of Classic Articles.* New York: Garland Publishing Inc., 1985.

A compilation of classic articles on media selection models, displaying the evaluation and development of media models.

302. Duffy, Ben. *Advertising Media and Markets.* New York: Garland Publishing Inc., 1985. Reprint.

Focuses on media selection in this book. Beginning with the creation of an advertisement, Duffy then analyzes various media and gives tips for evaluating advertisement effectiveness.

303. Fajen, Stephen R. "More for Your Money from the Media," *Harvard Business Review*, September-October 1978: 113-121.

By examining the history and future of media pricing, this article attempts to show advertisers how to get more from their advertising dollar spent in the media market. Topics explored include strengths and weaknesses of radio and television, the change of magazines to a more selective audience, and variations in newspaper intended to increase the value of individual ads.

304. Gardner, Fred. "Software Breakthrough," *Marketing and Decisions* May 1984: 70-71, 114-16.

Describes two personal computer software packages, IMS' MediaPak and Telmar's Micronet, which aid media planning by plotting the best reach and frequency combinations for the media dollar.

305. Gensch, Dennis H. "Computer Models in Advertising Media Selection." *Journal of Marketing Research*, November 1968: 414-24.

Surveys the various computer-aided media decision models including linear and nonlinear programming, iteration, dynamic programming, heuristic models and simulation models, describing the strengths and faults of each. Of these six, the author finds the heuristic and simulation models most promising.

306. Hall, Robert W. *Media Math: Basic Techniques of Media Evaluation*. Lincolnwood, Illinois: Business Books, 1987.

Reviews basic math as applied to media evaluation. Averaging, indexing, weighting and figuring costs are discussed. Includes exercises and self tests.

\* Heflin, Debora T. A. and Robert C. Haygood. "Effects of Scheduling on Retention of Advertising Messages." Cited above as item 126.

307. Kaaty, Ronald B. "Media Connections in a Changing Consumer Environment," *Journal of Advertising Research* April/May 1986: RC3-RC7.

Discusses the changing nature of the television medium and the implications of these changes for the advertising industry. The changes and changing elements discussed include the consumer, cable systems, commercial "zapping," the marketplace and shorter length commercials.

308. Kleppner, Otto and Irving Settel. *Exploring Advertising*, Englewood Cliffs, New Jersey: Prentice-Hall, Inc., 1970.

A collection of articles by different authors compiled into the categories of purposes of advertising, costing advertising, media planning, research and management.

309. Kreshel, Peggy J., Kent M. Lancaster, and Margaret A. Toomey. "How Leading Advertising Perceives Effective Reach and Frequency," *Journal of Advertising* 14 (3, 1985): 32-38, 51.

Reports the results of survey data concerning the media planning techniques used by major advertising agencies. Specific attention is paid to the use of communication effects data in formulating media plans.

310. Krugman, Dean M. "Evaluating the Audiences of the New Media," *Journal of Advertising* 14 (4, 1985): 21-27.

Discusses the new media, including cable television and other new technologies. A model is presented which analyzes audience similarities and differences between new and conventional media. The future of cable advertising is also discussed.

311. Kurzbard, Gary and Lawrence C. Soley. "Estimating Newspaper Cumulative Audiences," *Journal of Advertising* 14 (2, 1985): 57-61.

Presents a regression model which estimates the two-issue cumulative audience of a newspaper when the average issue audience and population of the newspaper's market area are known. This figure can be used to calculate the effective reach of a newspaper advertising schedule.

312. Lancaster, Kent M., Peggy J. Kreshel, and Joya R. Harris. "Estimating the Impact of Advertising Media Plans: Media Executives Describe Weighting and Timing Factors," *Journal of Advertising* 15 (3, 1986): 21-29, 45.

Focuses on how leading advertising agencies use effective reach theory when developing media plans. Also presented are alternative definitions of effective reach and rationale supporting the use of various time intervals for media plan evaluation.

\* Lucas, D. B. and C. E. Benson. *Psychology for Advertisers.* Cited above as item 130.

313. Lucas, Darrell B. and Steuart H. Britt. *Measuring Advertising Effectiveness.* New York: Garland Publishing Inc., 1985. Reprint.

A comprehensive work on creative and media research. The first help of the book discusses the techniques of planning and evaluating advertisements, devoting a separate chapter to each evaluative method. The second half discusses media concepts, including characteristics of the audiences of the different media.

\* *Marketing and Media Decisions.* New York: Decision Publications, Inc., 1965-present.

Published monthly, this journal is designed for those professionals involved in media planning. Cited above as item 188.

314. McGann, Anthony F. and John Thomas Russell. *Advertising Media: A Managerial Approach.* Homewood, Illinois: Richard D. Irwin, Inc., 1981.

A comprehensive guide and text covering the various media available. The managerial viewpoint is used as the strengths and weaknesses of each medium are analyzed.

315. Michman, Ronald D. and Donald W. Jugenheimer. *Strategic Advertising Decisions: Selected Selected Readings.* Columbus, Ohio: Grid, Inc., 1976.

    A collection of classic and contemporary articles which demonstrate advertising decision making. Decisions are discussed in the areas of creativity, media planning, international advertising and public policy.

316. Naples, Michael J. *Effective Frequency: The Relationship Between Frequency and Advertising Effectiveness.* Chicago: Crain Books, 1987.

    Discusses the effective use of frequency in an environment of increasing media costs and explains how to tailor media plans to the specific needs of the advertiser. Naples draws on case studies and the advice of several media experts.

317. Papazian, Ed. "Which Medium Is Toughest to Buy?" *Marketing and Media Decisions* June 1984: 84-86.

    Discusses the many details involved in media buying. In response to a claim that newspaper space is hardest to buy, a comparison is made between network and spot television, magazines, and newspapers. Spot television is judged to be most exacting.

\*   *Papers of the American Association of Advertising Agencies.* Cited above as item 22.

\*   Pattis, S. William. *Advertising Careers.* Cited above as item 261.

\*   Quelch, John A., and Paul W. Farris. *Cases in Advertising and Promotion Management.* Cited above as item 218.

318. Ries, Al. "What Ad Planners Learn from War." *Marketing Times.* May/August 1979. 29-31.

Media planning involves analyzing the media selection as a battle plan. Media planners start with print as the infantry, television as the air force, outdoor as the artillary, radio as the army, and direct mail as the airborne attack. Military strategy can be transferred to media planning.

319. Rust, Ronald T. *Advertising Media Models: A Practical Guide.* Lexington, Massachusetts: Lexington Books, 1986.

A concise how-to guide to media selection. The author discusses where to find information for decision making. The best media decision models available are also explained, including reach models, duplication models, frequency of exposure models, media selection models, viewing choice models, ratings models, and program scheduling models.

320. Rust, Roland T., George Haley, and Mukesh Bajaj. "Efficient and Inefficient Media for Political Campaign Advertising." *Journal of Advertising* 13 (3, 1984): 45-49.

Compares newspaper, magazine, and television media for effectiveness in reaching voters. Readership of newspapers and magazines is more positively related to voter participation than television viewing, except that the heaviest television viewers are least likely to vote.

321. Rust, Roland T., Robert P. Leone, and Mary R. Zimmer. "Estimating the Duplicated Audience of Media Vehicles in National Advertising Schedules." *Journal of Advertising* 15 (3, 1986): 30-37.

Evaluates the best available methods for estimating audience duplication of various media. New models are proposed and tested which estimate audience duplication of different episodes of a television program and within different target markets.

322. Schultz, Don E., Dennis Martin, and William P. Brown. *Strategic Advertising Campaigns*, Chicago: Crain Books, 1986.

The marketing concept is used in this book to tie together the steps in the development and presentation of a strong successful advertising campaign, including research, problem definition, situation analysis and campaign evaluation. Sections discuss production of creative and media plans, organization, presentation, evaluation, merchandising and promotion. Illustration, bibliography and index are included.

323. Simon, Julian L. *The Management of Advertising*. Englewood Cliffs, New Jersey: Prentice-Hall, Inc., 1971.

A heavily media oriented book which discusses research methods for media selection, planning and evaluation. One unit is devoted to the estimation of sales-response functions. Another discusses managerial decision making regarding budget allocation, media schedule selection and advertisement construction. A case study in the concluding chapters integrates and summarizes the preceding chapters.

* Sissors, Jack Z., and William B. Goodrich. *Media Planning Workbook: With Discussions and Problems*, Second Edition. Cited above as item 222.

* Sissors, Jack Z., and Jim Surmanek. *Advertising Media Planning*, Second Edition. Cited above as item 223.

324. Soley, Lawrence C. and Leonard N. Reid. "Satisfaction with the Information and Value of Magazine and Television Advertising," *Journal of Advertising* 12 (3, 1983): 27-31.

Examines consumer satisfaction with the informational value of magazine and television advertising. Concludes that 1) consumers are more satisfied with the informational value of magazine ads than television ads; 2) blacks are more satisfied with both types of advertising than whites; and 3) middle income consumers are more satisfied with both types of advertising than are high and low income consumers.

* Stone, Bob. *Successful Direct Marketing Methods*, Third Edition. Cited below as item 442.

325. "Studying the Advertising Media." *Supermarketing*, July 1970: 30-43.

    The articles in this issue discuss the supermarketer's use of various media including television, radio, point of purchase, outdoor, and print.

326. Surmanek, Jim. *Media Planning: A Practical Guide*. Chicago: Crain Books, 1986.

    This book is a practical guide to the fundamentals of media available to the advertiser. The author is a vice-president of a leading advertising agency.

327. Surmanek, Jim. *Media Planning: A Quick and Easy Guide*. Chicago: Crain Books: 1983.

    A handbook designed to provide maximum information on the fundamentals of media planning with a minimal amount of time involved. Elements of the media plan are discussed along with ideas of what it takes to make advertising more effective.

328. "A Systemized Approach to Media Selection in European Markets," *Industrial Marketing*, October 1975: 77- 78, 82.

    The author proposes a six-step media selection model: (1) market screening, (2) plotting target groups, (3) weighting targets, (4) strategy planning, (5) media selection, (6) evaluating results.

* Tipper, Harry, George Burton Hotchkiss, Harry L. Hollingworth, and Frank Alvah Parsons. *Advertising, Its Principles and Practices*. Cited above as item 224.

329. Wimmer, Roger D., and Joseph R. Dominick. *Mass Media Research: An Introduction*, Second Edition. Belmont, California: Wadsworth Publishing, 1987.

A mass media research book which devotes units to the research process, research approaches, basic statistics, research applications, and analyzing and reporting data. Among the research applications is a chapter on advertising including copy testing, media research, campaign assessment and public relations research.

*Print Media*

\* *Advertising Doesn't Cost...and Other Lies.* Cited above as item 287.

330. "Best of Class: NORMA Ad Winners," *Stores* January 1987: 102-106.

Exhibits the winners of awards for best newspaper retails advertisment for the year 1986. The competition was sponsored by the National Retail Merchants Association and the Newspaper Advertising Bureau. Categories of ads include institutional, public service, use of color, and sizes of stores. Illustrated.

331. Caples, John. *Advertising Ideas: A Practical Guide To Methods That Make Advertisements Work.* New York: Garland Publishing, Inc., 1985. Reprint.

A highly successful copywriter, Caples dissects 100 "successful" print advertisements, analyzing their various elements including headlines, copy and layout.

\* Calkins, Earnest Elmo, and Ralph Holden. *Modern Advertising.* Cited above as item 4.

332. Chapman, Bert. "Color Me Black and White," *Graphic Arts Monthly* May 1986: 58-60.

Reports that magazine advertising has turned around with respect to color versus black and white. Whereas earlier the color ads were fewer and more noticed than black and white, now color has become more popular, and black and white ads are the contrasting ads. Many advertisers are returning to black and white to achieve contrast.

333. "Color in Advertising," *Advertising Age*, 29 November 1965, various pages.

This issue of *Advertising Age* deals mostly with color in advertising. It contains 16 pages of color illustrations featuring color in outdoor, newspaper, magazines, and television. One section deals with packaging and another section includes statistical data on color in advertising.

334. Console, John. "Get out of Your Office and Sell," *SCAN* (reprinted from *Editor and Publisher*) April 1986: 6-7.

Discusses the need for newspaper advertising executives to improve their sales records. The author briefly suggests ways for newspapers to increase advertising sales.

335. *Editor and Publisher, The Fourth Estate*. New York: Editor and Publisher Company, 1901-present.

A journal of the newspaper industry which contains a wide variety of articles concerned with newspaper production and management.

336. Ferguson, Leonard W. "The Importance of the Mechanical Features of an Advertisement." *Journal of Applied Psychology* 19 (1935): 521-26.

An early study of newspaper advertising effectiveness as a function of the ad's mechanical features. The author concludes, based on survey data, that there is no significant relationship between size and position of an ad and its attention value. Ad readership and attention values are closely related to the day of the week and the sex of the reader.

337. Fletcher, Alan D. *Yellow Pages Advertising*. Chesterfield, Missouri: American Association of Yellow Pages Publishers, 1986.

Discusses the yellow pages and an informational, unobtrusive advertising medium. The development of the medium, how consumers use the yellow pages and how an advertiser can use the yellow pages are included as in production of yellow pages advertisements.

338. Gersh, Debra. "Outserts Are the New In Way to Pick up Additional Ad Dollar." *Editor and Publisher* May 3, 1986: 36.

Reports on a new development in print advertising- the "outserts" which is an ad card wrapped around the outside on a newspaper's Sunday television book. Outserts offer an advantage of increased exposure over conventional ads.

339. Gersh, Debra. "What Print Ads Are Effective?" *Editor and Publisher* May 3, 1986: 20-22.

Discusses newspaper advertising research and presents several advantages of print over television advertising. These advantages of print include active audience involvement, no electronic zapping, and the ineffectiveness of the fifteen-second television commercial.

\*   Glessing, Robert J. and William P. White. *Mass Media: The Invisible Enviroment*. Cited above as item 85.

340. "The Good and Bad of Newspaper Inserts or What's in It for Me?" *Direct Marketing*, June 1972: 38-46.

A panel discussion examines the advantages and disadvantages of the newspaper insert as part of the marketing mix. The aspects discussed include costs, the possibility of "insert clutter" and methods of testing new inserts.

* Graphic Arts Monthly, and the Printing Industry. New York: Technical Publishing, 1929-present.

   A technical journal for the printing industry. Cited above as item 171.

341. Guide to Quality Newspaper Reproduction. Washington, D.C.: American Newspaper Publishers Association; New York: Newspaper Advertising Bureau, 1986.

   Shows newspaper advertisers how to make their advertising most effective for the money in both black-and-white and color. Discusses copy, layout, artwork, photography and typography.

342. Hall, S. Roland. Retail Advertising and Selling. New York: Garland Publishing, Inc., 1985. Reprint.

   A comprehensive guide to retailing which covers all areas of retail selling. Included in the discussion are newspaper and outdoor advertising and copywriting.

343. Harmon, Robert R., Nabil Y. Razzouk, and Bruce L. Stern. "The Informational Content of Comparative Magazine Advertisements." Journal of Advertising 12 (4, 1984): 10-19.

   Reports the results of a content analysis of magazine advertisements intended to determine whether comparative advertisements contain more objective information than noncomparative ads. The comparative ads were shown to have greater information content.

344. Houston, Franklin S., and Diane Scott. "The Determinants of Advertising Page Exposure," Journal of Advertising 13 (2, 1984): 27-33.

Describes a model used to estimate the likelihood that a simple "average" advertising page will be exposed in medical journals. Factors affecting this model include: number of pages in a journal, frequency of publication, regularity of delivery and the density of the journal's advertising.

345. Jackson, Ralph W., and A. Parasuramon. "The Yellow Pages as an Advertising Tool for Small Business," Spring, 1986: 29-35.

Presents findings of a consumer survey regarding the use of yellow pages advertising. Their studies show the frequency of yellow pages use by consumers, the types of businesses sought in the yellow pages, and the relationship between size and position of the ad and consumer response. An interesting finding is that two-thirds of the respondents used the yellow pages rather than the white pages when they wanted the phone number of a specific place of business.

346. Jacoby, Stephen. "Newspaper, How To Get Something Extra," SCAN (condensed from Marketing and Media Decisions) March 1986: 1-2.

Discusses the advantages of the newspaper medium for reaching affluent, educated adults and gives statistics. The author suggests that newspapers should do a better job of selling themselves.

\*   Kalish, David. "All the Print That's Fit News." Cited above as item 281.

347. Kaufman, Lionel. "Fifty-Five Years in Print, from 'B. T.' to A. T.,'" SCAN (condensed from Marketing and Media Decisions) February, 1986: 5-9.

A broad discussion of television's effect on newspapers and magazines. The author discusses the actions taken by magazines in defense, including specialization and demographic research.

\*   Kurzbard, Gary and Lawrence C. Soby. "Estimating Newspaper Cumulative Audiences." Cited above as item 310.

348. Leigh, James H. "Recall and Recognition Performance for Umbrella Print Advertisements," Journal of Advertising 13 (4, 1984): 5-18, 30.

Umbrella advertisements involve promoting several products linked by a common theme in an attempt to achieve efficiency. The author investigates the conditions under which the use of umbrella ads is most appropriate.

* Lewis, Herschell Gordon. How to Make Your Advertising Twice as Effective at Half the Cost. Cited above as item 283.

349. Lorimor, E. S. "Classified Advertising: A Neglected Medium," *Journal of Advertising*, Winter 1977: 17- 25.

Classified advertising is a major medium and makes more money than advertising in newspapers. With this in mind, the author deliberates the social role and governmental regulation of classified advertising.

* Lucas, D. B., and C. E. Benson. *Psychology for Advertisers*. Cited above as item 130.

350. Lynn, Jerry R. "Newspaper Ad Impact in Nonmetropolitan Markets," *Journal of Advertising Research*. 21 (August 1981): 13-19.

Attempts to define the effectiveness of nonmetropolitan newspaper advertising on the nonmetropolitan newspaper audience.

351. Madden, Charles S., Majorie J. Caballero, and Shinya Matsukubo. "Analysis of Information Content in U.S. and Japanese Magazine Advertising." *Journal of Advertising*. 15 (3, 1986): 38-45.

Compares the content of U.S. and Japanese magazine advertising to determine relative levels of information content based on type of magazine, kind of information, product type, and the size of the ad. Japanese ads were found to be generally more informative than U.S. ads.

\* Madden, Thomas J., and Marc G. Weinberger. "The Effects of Humor on Attention in Magazine Advertising." Cited above as item 132.

\* Moskin, J. Robert. *The Case for Advertising.* Cited above as item 256.

352. Ogilvy, David and Joel Raphaelson. "Research on Advertising Techniques That Work -- and Don't Work." *Harvard Business Review*, 60 (July/August 1982): 14-18.

    Presents a review on the effectiveness of the different approaches in magazine ads and television commercials. The ability of different techniques such as slice-of-life, testimonials, problem solution and demonstration to change brand preference, attract attention and increase recall are discussed here.

353. Peeler, Bill. "Avoid the 61 Print Ad Pitfalls," *Business Marketing* February 1987: 106-111.

    Discusses sixty-one common print advertising mistakes which will impair an advertisement's effectiveness if not avoided. The mistakes deal with all components of a print ad, including headlines, body copy, style, visuals, color, layout, order forms, typography, and placement.

354. Peloquin, Florence. "Print Advertising -- How to Buy It from One Who Sells It," *Direct Marketing*, September 1975: 42ff.

    Analyzes the different aspects of using magazines to advertise mail-order items. It is argued that magazines may be used to prospect for first time customers. Also considers whether magazines sold in newstands are better for mail-order items than magazines sold by subscription.

\* Perlongo, Bob, editor. *Early American Advertising.* Cited above as item 24.

355. Pfaff, Fred, and Patrick Kelly, editors. "1985 Brand Leaders in Newspapers," *SCAN* (condensed from *Marketing and Media Decisions*) July 1986: 6-7.

    National expenditures for newspaper advertising grew by 8.8% between 1984 and 1985. Pfaff discusses reasons for that increase and projected future increases.

\* Pollay, Richard W. "The Subsidizing Sizzle: A Descriptive History of Print Advertising, 1900- 1980." Cited above as item 25.

356. Rogers, Jason. *Building Newspaper Advertising.* New York: Garland Publishing, Inc., 1985. Reprint.

    Discusses the use of newspapers as an advertising medium and the factors which contribute to a print advertisement's success. The roles of the newspaper and the advertising agency in creating and producing effective ads.

357. Salinger, Bernie. "Learning the Language Minimizes Screwups." *SCAN* (condensed from *Advertising Techniques*) 1986: 10-12.

    The technical industry of printing has its own language, and advertising agency personnel need to know enough to communicate with printers. The author tells how to gain this knowledge.

358. Sentman, Mary Alice. *Reallocation of Advertising Funds in Changing Newspaper Markets.* Ph.D. dissertation. Indiana University, 1984.

    Analyzes the impact of newspaper failure on the budgets of advertisers. Advertisers in cities which have recently lost a newspaper thus (becoming monopoly newspaper markets) were surveyed as to how they reallocated their newspaper advertising funds. Most remained in print media.

\* *SRDS Consumer Magazine and Agri-Media Rate and Data.* Cited above as item 155.

\* *SRDS Newspaper Rates and Data.* Cited above as item 156.

359. Weinstein, Steve. "Retail Advertising: Looking for a Look," *SCAN* (condensed from *Madison Avenue*) July 1986: 15-16.

    Discusses the weakness of retail advertising's use of price promotion in newspaper ads. The author suggests that the store should market itself as a brand.

360. Weisberger, Fran. "Technological Advancements in Newspapers." *SCAN* (condensed from *Marketing and Media Decisions*) October 1985: 1-2.

    Discusses the increased use of color in newspaper advertisements. Color commands more attention than black-and-white, and technological advances have made easier the use of color in newspapers. Includes findings of research of the use of color.

\* Whetmore, Edward Jay. *Mediamerica: Form, Content and Consequence of Mass Communication.* Third Edition. Cited above as item 226.

361. "Why Magazines Are Coming on Stronger," *Business Week*, 25 October 1976: 140, 142, 146.

    Advertisers are breaking the routine of using television without looking first at other media. Contributing to this may be the rise of television rates, limited time availability, and program violence. The advantages of using magazine over television advertising are discussed in this article.

362. Woodside, Arch G., and Ilkka A. Ronkainen. "Travel Advertising: Newspapers versus Magazines," *Journal of Advertising Research*, 22 (June/July 1982): 39-43.

More travel advertising dollars go to magazines than to newspapers, and in this article, the authors discuss and question this strategy. Considering revenue per inquiry and cost per inquiry, the results of a survey by the authors indicate that newspapers outdo magazines on black and white as well as color campaigns.

*Electronic Media*

The use of sound and/or sight has unique capabilities of reaching specialized audiences with specialized products. The two major areas of this electronic media are television and radio. Specific areas that are included are zapping of messages, clutter, cable television, videocassette recorders, videotex cinema advertising, audience characteristics, sponsorship, audience measurement, and media scheduling.

363. Aaker, David A. "Controlling Adjacent Commercials," *SCAN* (condensed from *Advertising Age*) June 1986: 21-23.

Briefly presents the results of experiments which attempted to establish a relationship between adjacent commercials. A comercial's effectiveness is influenced by the type of commercials preceding it.

364. Aaker, David A. and Donald Norris. "Characteristics of TV Commercials Perceived as Informative," *Journal of Advertising Research*. 22 (April/May 1982): 61-70.

The importance of informative advertising is discussed. The informative value of television advertising is focused on as well as the characteristics of commercials that prime time viewers see as informative and relevant.

\*   Abrahams, Howard P. "Retail Advertising: Radio Break Through in the '60's, TV in the '70's." Cited above as item 1.

\*   *Advertising Doesn't Cost...And Other Lies.* Cited above as item 288.

365. Alten, Stanley R. *Audio in Media,* Second Edition. Belmont, California: Wadsworth Publishing, 1986.

    Discusses the principles, equipment and production of sound in the mass media. A good reference guide for the advertiser who is concerned with radio and television production.

366. "Another Option: Regional Net TV." *Media Decisions,* October 1976: 132-134.

    This article compares the advantages of using network time on a regional basis against using like coverage on a spot basis. Regional buying offers a cost advantage but necessitates the need for advance committments that aren't needed with spot buying.

367. Armer, Alan A. *Directing Television and Film.* Belmont, California: Wadsworth Publishing, 1986.

    Armer combines theory and practice in this book. Written primarily for the beginning director, the book contains a chapter on directing commercials. A good source book for the advertiser.

368. Austin, Bruce A. "Cinema Screen Advertising: An Old Technology with New Promise For Consumer Marketing," *Journal of Consumer Marketing,* Vol. 3 No. 1 Winter 1986: 45-56.

    Discusses the advantages of cinema advertising including population segmentation and a captive attentive audience.

369. Baldwin, Huntley. *Creating Effective TV Commercials.* Chicago: Crain Books, 1986.

Traces the steps showing how commercials came about. It describes what is necessary for a good commercial, how to develop a primary selling idea, and how to implement it. It also includes film language and structure, storyboard analysis, and expression of ideas in visual form.

370. Barban, Arnold M. and Dean M. Krugman. "Cable Television and Advertising: An Assessment," *Journal of Advertising*, Fall 1978: 4-8.

    The policies of the Federal Communication Commission are discussed. Also reviewed is the position of the cable industry in relation to advertising.

371. Barr, David Samuel. *Advertising on Cable: A Practical Guide for Advertisers*. Englewood Cliffs, New Jersey: Prentice-Hall, Inc., 1985.

    Illustrates the usefulness of cable advertising for both recreational and local advertisers, giving guidelines for creating successful cable commercials and campaigns. Specialized topics, such as political advertising, co-op advertising and data channels are discussed.

\*   Bello, Daniel C., Robert W. Pitts and Michael J. Etzel. "The Communication Effects of Controversial Sexual Content in Television Programs and Commercials." Cited above as item 117.

\*   Beltramini, Richard F. "The Impact of Infomercials: Perspectives of Advertisers and Advertising Agencies." Cited above as item 231.

372. Bogart, Leo, and Charles Lehman. "The Case of the 30-Second Commercial." *Journal of Advertising Research* February/March 1983: 11-19.

Presents a before-and-after comparison of commercial performance to evaluate the effect of the switch from 30-second to 60-second commercials.

373. Book, Albert C., Norman D. Cary, and Stanley J. Tannenbaum. *The Radio and Television Commercial.* Chicago: Crain Books, 1978.

    A guide to producing effective television and radio advertisements. Fifty exercises for improving copy writing skills are included, as are examples of scripts and storybooks.

374. "The Bounds of Barter Are Hard to Find," *Broadcasting,* 6 May 1974: 22-27.

    Discusses bartering in the mass media, where companies give stations programs in return for advertising time. The rationale of bartering is that the advertiser can get more for its money, and the article predicts that barter will become less prevalent in the future. The specific programs bartered and criticisms of the practice are also discussed.

375. Bronson, Gail. "Ads in Movies? You're Already Watching Them," *U.S. News & World Report,* August 20, 1984: 43-44.

    Discusses publicity of products in films. Various ways that product placement brokers put products into movies as props or as dialogue are discussed.

\*   Bush, Alan J. and James H. Leigh. "Advertising on Cable Versus Traditional Networks." Cited above as item 293.

\*   Cannon, Hugh M. "Media-Market Matching versus Random-Walk' in Television Media Selection." Cited above as item 295.

\*   Cannon, Hugh M. "A Method for Estimating Target Market Ratings in Television Media Selection." Cited above as item 296.

\* Caples, John. *How to Make Your Advertising Make Money.* Cited above as item 143.

\* "Color in Advertising." Cited above as item 333.

376. Darpetti, Anthon. "Radio Sales Techniques for the rest of the '80's." *Broadcasting* April 1, 1985: 22.

    Discusses the necessity of instituting major account selling on both national and local levels in order to increase radio's share of dollars.

377. Day, Harry. "The Seven Deadly Sins." *SCAN* (condensed from *Advertising Age*) May, 1985: 8.

    Describes seven shortcomings of both the agency and advertiser which can ruin the making of a television commercial and suggests ways to avoid them.

378. Demkowych, Christine. "Music on the Upswing in Advertising," *Advertising Age.* March 31, 1986: 55.

    Discusses the advent of the use of pop music in commercials. With the increased use of music in commercials, several agencies have established music departments to service industry demands.

379. Donious, James F. "Campaign Simulation Via Multiple Exposure On-Air Copy Testing," *Journal of Advertising Research*, 23 (April/May 1983): 35- 39.

    Presents the results of experiments to determine the cumulative effectiveness of straight sell and mood advertising. The author holds that straight sell has greater power through multiple exposures than mood advertising.

\* Duetsch, Larry L. "Advertising and Profitability Among Large Industrial Corporations." Cited above as item 40.

380. Duncan, Calvin P., and James Nelson. "Effects of Humor in a Radio Advertising Experiment." *Journal of Advertising* 14 (2, 1985): 33-40, 64.

Examines the impact of perceived humor on nine advertising variables. Humor is shown to affect attention to the ad, liking the ad, liking the product, and irritation. Also finds that attitude toward advertisement mediates humor's effect on product preference and intuition to buy.

381. Dunlap, William H. "Staying Tuned to Business -- Industrial Radio Advertising." *Business Marketing* October 1985: 104-106.

Discusses the popularity of radio among business-to- business marketers. Three reasons are cited including the popularity of radio-listening, special formats of stations and cost effectiveness.

382. Dygert, Warren Benson. *Radio as an Advertising Medium*. New York: Garland Publishing, Inc., 1985 Reprint.

Contains discussions of the various facets of radio advertising, including radio time, broadcasting tools, competition, script writing, censorship, ratings, tests, surveys and foreign broadcasting. Based on this discussion, the author assesses the possibilities of radio as a communication vehicle for advertising.

383. Edwards, Morris. "Picture Brightens for USA Videotex/Teletext." *Communications News*, 20 (August 1983): 98-102.

An overview of the videotex-teletext media including the history and prospects for the future. Includes results of several research studies.

384. Eicoff, Al. *Eicoff on Broadcast Direct Marketing*. Chicago: Crain Books, 1987.

Stresses a simple approach to direct marketing through the broadcast media. The author's three step approach includes telling the customer about the product, showing that the product works, and telling the customer where to buy. Several special topics are discussed, including how to buy broadcast time, test marketing, evaluation, sales resistance, and cable advertising.

385. Felsenthal, Norman, G. Wayne Shamo, and John R. Bittner. "A Comparison of Award-Winning Radio Commercials and Their Day-to-Day Counterparts," *Journal of Broadcasting*, Summer 1971: 309-315.

Compares "CLIO" award winning commercials with those not judged as good and identifies characteristics of the commercial production are made: Use dramatization rather than straight dialogue. Make the sponsor identification suspenseful. Avoid overidentification of the sponsor. Use stylistic indices in writing the advertisements.

386. Fruit, Fran. "Look What They've Done to my Song, Ma." *SCAN* (condensed from *Advertising Age*) June, 1986: 9-10.

Discusses the use of popular music from the 1960's in commercials in order to appeal to the nostalgic senses of baby boomers.

387. Gates, Fliece. "Further Comments on the Miscomprehension of Televised Advertisements." *Journal of Advertising* 15 (1, 1986): 4-9.

Tests the performance of true-false and multiple choice questions for measuring recognition of television commercials and the effect of type of television ad appeal on measurements of recognition and miscomprehension.

388. Gelb, Betsy D., and George M. Zinkhan. "Humor and Advertising Effectiveness After Repeated Exposure to a Radio Commercial." *Journal of Advertising* 15 (2, 1986): 15-20, 34.

Tests a model relating perceived humor to measures of advertising effectiveness with regard to brand name recall, attitude toward the brand, stated purchase probability and actual brand choice. Humor was found to be negatively related to recall and positively related to attitude toward the brand.

\* Glessing, Robert J., and William P. White. *Mass Media The Invisible Environment.* Cited above as item 85.

389. Harper, Ron C. "Making Better Commercials." *Radio Only*, April 1985: 44.

   Explains how to improve radio advertising by working with the four elements of radio advertising -- sound effects, voice, music and the idea.

390. Harvey, Michael G., and James T. Rothe. "Video-Cassette Recorders: Their Impact on Viewers and Advertisers," *Journal of Advertising Research* December 1985/January 1986: 19-27.

   Examines the importance of the popularity of VCR's for advertisers. Also included is a discussion of how the VCR has modified viewing habits and how VCR owners use their equipment.

391. Heeter, Carrier, and Bradley Greenberg. "Profiling the Zappers." *Journal of Advertising Research* April/May 1985: 15-19.

   Describes the phenomenon of zapping of television commercials. Special focus is on the viewing behavior of those viewers who zap commercials. The authors state that commercial avoidance is not the primary cause of zapping.

\* Heighton, Elizabeth J., and Don R. Cunningham. *Advertising in the Broadcast Media.* Cited above as item 210.

\* Henry Brian, editor. *British Television Advertising: The First Thirty Years.* Cited above as item 12.

392. "Hints on Getting More Free Publicity," *Radio Only*, August 1985: 33.

Discusses publicity strategies for radio stations, including promotion ideas and guidelines from radio stations managers.

393. Hoyer, Wayne D., Rajendra K. Srivastana, and Jacob Jacoby. "Sources of Miscomprehension in Television Advertising," *Journal of Advertising* 13 (2, 1984): 17-26.

    Explores the factors leading to miscomprehension of television commercials. Differences in receivers of the message and in the content of the message both account for miscomprehension. The implications of this study for message development are discussed.

394. "In-Flight Ads: A New Business Takes Off." *Business Week*, No. 2787 (25 April 1983): 106.

    Discusses the escalation of advertising on in-flight movies. Fifteen major airlines now accept advertising. This medium offers less clutter than radio or television and the opportunity to reach a business audience.

395. James, Watson S. "The New Electronic Media: An Overview." *Journal of Advertising Research*, 23 (August/September 1983): 33-37.

    Provides a good description of the electronic media available to consumers and advertisers. The author goes into topics such as subscription television, cable television, direct broadcast satellites and multipoint distribution service.

396. Johnson, Keith F. "Cinema Advertising." *Journal of Advertising*, 10 (No. 4, 1981): 11-19.

    Cinema advertising proves to be effective for improving product and advertising awareness, shifts in image and opinion, and carryover recall. Theater advertising is capable of higher quality presentation than television as well as other advantages discussed in this article.

\*   Jordan, J. J. "Accountability in Media?" Cited above as item 244.

* Kaaty, Ronald B. "Media Connections in a Changing Consumer Environment." Cited above as item 307.

397. Kaplan, Barry M. "Zapping -- The Real Issue is Communication." *Journal of Advertising Research* April/May 1985: 9-12.

    Explores the issue of zapping and how it disrupts the advertising communications process.

* Kunkel, Dale Lyman. *Children's Understanding of Television Advertising: The Impact of Host- Selling.* Cited above as item 93.

398. Leigh, Mathew Andrew. "Nibble. Nibble. Nibble," *SCAN* (condensed from *Madison Avenue*) September 1986: 21-23.

    Examines the erosion of advertiser and viewer support of network television. Three reasons are cited for the networks' loss, including their mass appeal, the loss of appeal to women, high costs and the clutter of the 15 second commercial.

* Lewis, Herschell Gordon. *How to Make Your Advertising Twice as Effective at Half the Cost.* Cited above as item 284.

399. Loesch, K. Linford. "Turning on Radio Advertising for Banks," *The Bankers Magazine*, Summer 1971: 89- 95.

    This article introduces radio as an effective medium for bank advertising. The merits of radio as a medium are discussed, as are methods for bankers to use information which is already in their possession to identify markets.

400. MacLachlan, James, and Priscilla LaBarbera. "Time Compressed TV Commercials." *Journal of Advertising Research*, August 1978: 11-15.

    Time compression may be a useful managerial tool according to this article. It could increase interest where the message may be slower paced and the interest low. Also, the attention power of commercials may be increased.

* McMahon, Harry W. "BST: A Way to Get Your Creative Problem out of the Revolving Door." Cited as item 489.

401. Meeske, Milan D., and R. C. Norris. *Copywriting for the Electronic Media: A Practical Guide.* Belmont, California: Wadsworth Publishing, 1987.

    Discusses all types of copywriting for broadcast media and devotes separate chapters to the writing of television and radio commercials and public service announcements.

402. Mitchell, Maurice B. "Second Time Around: Words About Radio Still Ring True," *Broadcasting*, September 10, 1973: 22-23.

    Discusses five timeless hints for improving radio effectiveness: knowing objectives, program targeting, regularly promoting the best products, using the right copy and coordinating the advertising.

* Moskin, J. Robert. *The Case for Advertising.* Cited above as item 256.

403. "Murdock's Sky Channel is Turning Advertisers On," *Business Week*, March 31, 1986: 82.

    The success story of Rupert Murdock's Sky Channel satellite television network. In three years, Murdock has captured a European audience of 5.5 million in thirteen countries. The growth of the network has begun to attract international advertisers in great numbers.

404. Nielsen, Arthur C. Jr. "The Outlook for Electronic Media." *Journal of Advertising Research*, 22 (December 1982/January 1983): 9-16.

Data on basic cable and pay television trends as well as informations on the past, present and future of electronic media are given. Other topics discussed include teletext, videotext, direct broadcast satellites and multipoint distribution.

405. O'Donnell, Lewis B., Carl Hausman, and Philip Benoit. *Announcing: Broadcast Communicating Today.* Belmont, California: Wadsworth Publishing, 1987.

\* Ogilvy, David and Joel Raphaelson. "Research on Advertising Techniques That Work -- and Don't Work." Cited above as item 352.

406. O'Guinn, Thomas C., Ronald J. Faber, and Timothy P. Meyer. "Ethnic Segmentation in Spanish-Language Television." *Journal of Advertising* 14 (3, 1985): 63-66.

Discusses the use of Spanish-language broadcasting and presents a profile of Mexican-Americans who prefer Spanish-language television to English-language television. The implications of this profile for advertisers using an ethnic segmentatioin strategy are discussed.

407. Padley, Martin. "How Do You Use Radio -- for Price, Event, or Image?" *Stores*, October 1968: 16-20.

Considers retailers' increased use of radio advertising and the various radio strategies employed by retailers. The most popular objectives of radio advertisers include: stressing prices for special sales, promoting fashion for teenagers, maintaining popularity year round, and "blitzing" a market during a special promotion.

408. Pridgen, Dee. "Satellite Television Advertising and the Regulatory Conflict in Western Europe." *Journal of Advertising* 14 (1, 1985): 23-29, 56.

Reviews the growth of transnational television advertising in Western Europe and the conflicting advertising regulations of the European Economic Community which may hinder further growth. Current regulations and laws for harmonization are described.

409. Ray, Michael L. and Peter H. Webb. "Three Prescriptions for Clutter." *Journal of Advertising Research* February/March 1986: 69-77.

Suggests and describes several techniques for avoiding clutter in an increasingly cluttered television environment. Techniques discussed focus on research, testing, and scheduling.

410. Riter, Charles B., Phillip J. Balducci, and Donald McCollum. "Time Compression: New Evidence," *Journal of Advertising Research*, 22 (December 1982/January 1983): 39-43.

The effects of time compression on advertising are presented. The common arguments for time compression are discussed and the methodology is outlined. It is concluded in the three samples studied that compressed commercials show an improvement in brand awareness and recall but a loss in motivation.

411. Rosenthal, Edmond M. "Agencies Confront Creative Limitations of 15-Second Spots." *Television/Radio Age* June 23, 1986: 55-56, 86-90.

Surveys agency attitudes of the increased use of fifteen-second television commercials and how agencies produce them. Two ways of producing fifteen-second commercials are to condense thirty-second commercials and to create new commercials. Research findings show that the fifteen-second ads have lower recall and effectiveness than thirty-second commercials. The fifteen-second ads feature more hard sell and less emotion building than longer ads.

412. Schneider, Cy. *Children's Television: The Art, the Business, and How It Works.* Chicago: Crain Books, 1987.

Explains how to effectively direct marketing communications at children through television. Children's television advertising represents a $600 million a year business, and this work is helpful reading for anyone involved with this market.

413. Sherrid, Pamela. "Emotional Shorthand," *Forbes*, November 4, 1985: 214.

    Explains the use of pop music in commercials as a quick way to stir audience emotions. Certain emotions are inextricably tied to certain melodies, and music is used to link favorable emotions with a product. Music publishers' attitudes are favorable but tend to be adverse when original lyrics are replaced by product lyrics.

414. "Special Report: Radio Advertising," *Advertising Age* September 13, 1982: M1-M21.

    A special supplement featuring radio advertising. Articles report on the history of radio advertising, advertiser opinions about radio, creativity and copywriting, co-op advertising, and building a station's market shore.

\*   *SRDS Spot Radio Rates and Data*. Cited above as item 157.

\*   *SRDS Spot Television Rates and Data*. Cited above as item 158.

415. Stephens, Nancy. "The Effectiveness of Time- Compressed Television Advertisements with Older Adults," *Journal of Advertising* 11 (4, 1982): 48- 55, 76.

    Examines the effectiveness of time-compression advertisements with elderly adults. Recall from time-compressed ads diminishes as age increases. Normal television advertisements showed the same relationship between age and recall.

416. Stewart, David W. and David H. Furse. *Effective Television Advertising: A Study of 1000 Commercials*. Lexington, Massachusetts: Lexington Books, 1985.

    Presents the findings of a study of over 1000 commercials and their effect on consumers, identifying elements which influence memory and persuasion. For example, some commercials were found to be memorable but not persuasive, while others were persuasive but not memorable.

\* "Studying the Advertising Media." Cited above as item 325.

\* *Television/Radio Age*. New York: Television Editorial Coporation. 1952-present.

Published every two weeks, this periodical focuses on current happenings in the broadcasting field. Cited above as item 196.

417. Wainwright, Charles Anthony. *The Television Copywriter: How to Create Successful TV Commercials*. New York: Hastings House, 1966.

Wainwright, an advertising executive, writes a practical handbook covering all areas of television advertising production. A good source book for the novice in the television industry.

418. Weeks, Richard R. and William V. Marx. "Music's 'Power' for Television Advertising." *The Southern Journal of Business*, October 1968: 35-39.

Discusses the subjective area of musical effect in advertising. The article explains music's power for producing common behavior in groups of people and offers guidelines for the use of music. Music can be used to reinforce associative learning, to appeal to personality types, and in combination with color, visuals and copy to play upon emotions.

\* Whetmore, Edward Jay. *Mediamerica: Form, Content, and Consequence of Mass Communication*, Third Edition. Cited above as item 226.

419. White, Hooper. "Ad Groups Analyze Spiraling Production Costs," *SCAN* (condensed from *Advertising Age*) May 1986: 12-13.

The results of an Association of National Advertisers survey briefly describe the reasons why television commercial production costs have risen sharply in past years and give suggestions for cutting costs.

420. White, Hooper. *How to Produce Effective TV Commercials*, Second Edition. Chicago: Crain Books, 1986.

A comprehensive, practical guide for students and practitioners, this book covers in detail the production of a television commercial including editing and technological advances in the medium.

421. Willinger, Kurt. "Quest for the Zap-less Ad," *SCAN* (condensed from *Advertising Age*) February, 1986: 10-12.

Discusses "anti-advertising," advertising which does not follow the usual rules of advertising. Anti-advertising attempts to not look like advertising in order to avoid being ignored.

\* Zeigler, Sherilyn K. and Herbert H. Howard. *Broadcast Advertising*. Cited above as item 228.

422. Zettl, Herbert. *Television Production Handbook*, Fourth Edition. Belmont, California: Wadsworth Publishing, 1984.

Discusses the elements and techniques of television production, including the camera, lighting, sound, videotape and film, editing, producing, and directing. A good source book for the television advertiser.

## Direct Marketing and Out-of-Home Media

*Direct marketing* is a system whereby the advertiser uses the media to build a data base of customers. *Direct reponse* advertising is a message that asks for an immediate response. *Direct mail* is one form of direct response advertising. *Direct advertising* is any form of advertising issued directly to the customer through mail, salespeople, and other forms than the main media.

Out-of-home media can be in many forms: standardized outdoor structures (billboards), nonstandardized signs, and transit advertising. Transit advertising can be in the outside or inside of a moving vehicle or on station posters.

\*     *Advertising Doesn't Cost...and Other Lies.* Cited above as item 288.

423.  Agnew, Hugh E. *Outdoor Advertising.* New York: Garland Publishing, Inc., 1985. Reprint.

A comprehensive study of outdoor advertising. Topics discussed include the mechanics of outdoor advertising, the development of outdoor advertising, selling outdoor advertising, traffic and trade, art and outdoor advertising, and public policy. Case studies are included.

424.  Alsop, Ronald. "Soft Selling: Advertisers Make Their Pitches on Floppy Disks," *Wall Street Journal.* January 8, 1987: 17.

Describes a relatively new strategy used in the direct selling/mail advertising media which involves placing catalogs and sales brochures on floppy disks and distributing the disks to personal computer owners. Although expensive, the method allows the advantages of curiosity arousal, easy market segmentation, consumer interaction and the creation of a high-tech image for the product.

425.  Brann, Christon. *Direct Mail and Direct Reponse Promotion.* London: Kogan Page Limited, 1971.

A comprehensive guide to direct mail advertising, this book discusses methods of direct promotion, copywriting, production, the direct selling organization and international direct mail promotion.

* Cafferata, Mike. "Good Copy if Alive and Well." Cited as item 519.

* Calkins, Earnest Elmo, and Ralph Holden. *Modern Advertising*. Cited above as item 4.

* Caples, John. *How to Make Your Advertising Make Money*. Cited above as item 143.

426. Claus, Karen E. and R. James Claus. *The Sign User's Guide: A Marketing Aid*. Palo Alto, California: The Institute of Signage Research, 1978.

    Provides guidelines which will enable sign users to make effective and efficient use of their signs. The authors touch on large business but primarily write for the small business owner.

* "Color in Advertising." Cited above as item 332.

427. Crippen, John K. *Successful Direct-Mail Methods*. New York: Garland Publishing, Inc., 1985 Reprint.

    Discusses the fundamentals of a successful direct- mail campaign by discussing the elements of the mail- piece, the mailing campaign, mailing lists and test mailing. Direct mail is discussed as used both by itself and coupled with other advertising.

* Dugas, Christine. "'Ad Space' Now Has a Whole New Meaning." Cited as item 454.

* Eicoff, Al. *Eicoff on Broadcast Direct Marketing*. Cited above as item 384.

428. Forkan, James P. "Daylight Time Is Hurting Circulation of Outdoor." *Advertising Age*, 21 January 1974: 1, 73.

    Discusses the problem of late sunrise during daylight savings time and how it affects outdoor advertising. Displays which are

*The Institution of Advertising* *121*

only illuminated in evening hours cannot be seen during the morning rush hour.

* Green, Norma F. "Unusual Media Through the Years." Cited above as item 9.

* Hall, S. Roland. *Retail Advertising and Selling.* Cited above as item 342.

429. Henderson, Sally, and Robert Landau. *Billboard Art.* San Francisco, California: Chronicle Books, 1980.

    A pictorial chronicle of outdoor advertising, especially billboards. The artwork and content of outdoor advertisements are illustrated and discussed. Divided into five units based on chronology.

* Hodgson, Richard S. *Direct Mail and Mail Order Handbook.* Cited above as item 147.

* Katzenstein, Herbert, and William S. Sacks. *Direct Marketing.* Cited above as item 211.

* Larwood, Jacob, and John Camden Hotten. *The History of Signboards from the Earliest Times.* Cited above as item 16.

* Lewis, Herschell Gordon. *How to Make Your Advertising Twice as Effective at Half the Cost.* Cited above as item 284.

430. Lewis, Herschell Gordon. *More Than You Ever Wanted to Know About Mail Order Advertising.* Englewood Cliffs, New Jersey: Prentice-Hall, Inc., 1983.

    This handbook explains techniques that enhance the effectiveness and efficiency of mail order advertising. Included in the discussion are: media selection, mailing lists, copywriting and production, testing, and legal aspects.

431. Paslillo, Joseph G. P., and Peter Lorenze. "Marketing Incentives and Mail Questionnaire Reponse Rates," *Journal of Advertising* 13 (1, 1984): 46-49.

The results of an experiment indicate that the reponse rate to a mail questionnaire significantly increases when a one dollar incentive is enclosed. Promised incentives, including two dollars and lottery entries with awards of twenty, thirty, and fifty dollars in return for a completed questionnaire did not significantly improve the response rate.

432. Ross, Maxwell. "Direct Mail Produces Less Expensive, More Effective Sales Call," *Advertising and Sales Promotion*, April 1972: 110-111.

The practice of direct mail coordinated with a sales call has been shown to be more effective than an unannounced salesperson. Direct mail should give the customer enough information to spark an interest so that the salesperson will have a more receptive environment for a presentation.

433. Ross, Maxwell. "Opening Sentence Most Important Element in Direct Mail Writing," *Advertising and Sales Promotion*, February 1972: 72-73.

Because the opening sentence is the most important part of the letter, direct mail writers need to dedicate much of their time to this cause. The author gives six different ways to open the letter and also gives some helpful writing tips.

434. Ross, Maxwell. "Referral Names Are Best Prospects for Direct Mail." *Advertising and Sales Promotion*, June 1972: 134.

Concludes that referral names are the best prospects that can be found. Also, the more names that are asked for, the better the chance for a sale. Offering the customer a gift may increase the number of responses but the quality of the response may not.

435. Scripps-Howard News Service. "Nouveau-art Billboards Start Rolling in Business." *Arkansas Democrat* Newspaper. September 17, 1985: 1E.

   Discusses the comeback of the billboard as an advertising medium. Low cost and improved graphics are discussed as the advantages of billboards.

436. Self, Donald R., Jerry J. Ingram, and others. "Direct Response Advertising as an Element in the Promotional Mix." *Journal of Direct Marketing* Winter 1987: 50-55.

   Argues that direct response advertising should be considered as a separate element in the promotional mix because direct response advertising exists on a continuum between advertising and personal selling. Suggestions are made for maximizing the efficiency of direct response advertising.

437. Serafin, Raymond. "Where Rubber Meets the Air." *SCAN* (condensed from *Advertising Age*) October, 1985: 9- 10.

   A short account of Goodyear Tire and Rubber Company's use of the blimp as a medium. Briefly discussed are the history of the blimps, their use, their impact and B. F. Goodrich Company's counter advertising.

438. "Skytyping," *Public Relations Journal*, May 1985: 11- 12.

   Skytyping is a form of advertising which adds computer technology to traditional skywriting. Using several planes at once, skytyping produces messages at a rate of 20 to 25 letters per minute.

439. Snapp, Constance. "Direct Marketing, Step by Step," *SCAN* (condensed from *Marketing and Media Decisions*) August, 1986: 6-10.

A sixteen-step approach to direct marketing which covers planning, testing, creativity and production, salesmanship and prospect/customer relations.

440. "Special Report: Outdoor Advertising," *Advertising Age* December 12, 1986: 13-24.

    A special section reports on developments in outdoor advertising. Eight articles discuss new uses of the medium, newcomers to outdoor advertising, co-op advertising, new technologies, troubles faced by the medium, and international competitions. Illustrated.

441. Sroge, Maxwell. *How to Create Successful Catalogs.* Chicago: Crain Books, 1987.

    Reviews essential principles of effective catalog production, including art, copy and photography. Included are examples from hundreds of current successful catalogs. Guidelines are also given for complying with FTC regulations regarding copy content.

442. Stone, Bob. *Successful Direct Marketing Methods*, Third Edition. Chicago: Crain Books, 1984.

    Discusses techniques for getting started in direct marketing, in addition to media selection and creation and management of marketing. Included are illustrations and a self-quiz and pilot project after each chapter.

443. Stone, Bob. "Three Ways for Mail Advertisers to Boost Their Profits." *Advertising Age*, May 31, 1971: 33- 34.

    Reviews different ways to improve a firm's profits and yet not change any of its products or services. In direct mail, there are three elements of increased profits: better response, better markup, and lower advertising cost.

444. Strand, Patricia. "Chrysler Sees Car Sales by Mail," *SCAN* (reprinted from *Advertising Age*) August, 1985: 19.

Discusses the increasing prevalence of direct mail in automobile advertising and predicts that mail will replace the 30-second television commercial.

\* "Studying the Advertising Media." Cited above as item 324.

\* Taylor, Ronald A. "Billboard Still King of the Road." Cited above as item 109.

445. Tighe, John Francis. "A Good Mailing Needs a Good Offer," *SCAN* (condensed from *Advertising Age*) November, 1985: 22-3.

Discusses mail marketing and emphasizes the necessity of an offer to be contained in each mailing in order to generate response. Briefly discusses the use of reply cards, coupons and incentives to respond.

\* Tipper, Harry, George Burton Hotchkiss, Harry L. Hollingworth, and Frank Alrah Parsons. *Advertising, Its Principles and Practices*. Cited above as item 224.

446. Trainman, Stephen. "Video Music Marketing Big in N.Y." *Billboard*, 25 June 1977: 6, 45, 47.

Discusses the use of Spectacolor's 20 X 40 foot computerized billboard in New York City's Time's Square for video advertising of music. The automated and animated billboard promotes albums, concerts and television appearances.

*Sales Promotion and Supplementary Media*

Sales promotional tools are used to help produce and increase sales. These tools are often called "non- commissionable media." There are two major types of sales promotion: dealer promotion (push strategy), and consumer promotion (pull strategy). Such tools as point-of-purchase display, coupons, sponsorships, collateral materials, premiums, and co-op advertising. Supplementary media involves other forms of presenting the message to the prospective customer: specialty advertising, trade shows, directories and yellow pages, and cinema advertising.

447. Alsop, Ronald. "Companies Cram Ads in Stores to Sway Shopping Decisions." *Wall Street Journal.* August 22, 1985: 23.

   Two-thirds of buying decisions are made at the point of sale, thus there has been an increase in in- store advertising. Included are advertising on shopping carts, special clocks and in-store recorded messages.

448. "Appraising Coupons at Face Value." *SCAN* (condensed from *Marketing and Media Decisions*) February, 1986: 14-15.

   Briefly discusses several topics in couponing, including inflation and increased denominations, consumer attitudes and coupon clutter.

449. Bayers, Barry L. "Word of Mouth: The Indirect Effects of Marketing Efforts." *Journal of Advertising Research* June/July 1985: 31-39.

   Examines the effect of information obtained from other consumers on the purchase decision. A marketing strategy is outlined which incorporates the word of mouth medium.

\*   Bernhardt, Kenneth L. and Thomas C. Kinnear. *Cases in Marketing Management*, Third Edition. Cited above as item 36.

450. Bowman, Russ. "Sales Promotion." *Marketing and Media Decisions*, March 1986: 130-131.

   Discusses the growth of the promotional media of newspaper inserts and direct mail as alternatives to the broadcast media and magazines.

451. Bowman, Russ. "The Year in Coupons, 1986." *SCAN* (condensed from *Marketing and Media Decisions*) January, 1986: 5-6.

   Reports very briefly on the prospects and reasons for increased co-op couponing in 1986.

452. "Calling all Coupon Clippers." *Sales and Marketing Management* August 12, 1985: 47.

   Reports survey data concerning coupon distribution in 1984. Of 163 billion coupons issued by manufacturers, only four percent were redeemed. Also reports on a new marketing research technique designed to improve coupon response.

\*   Caples, John. *How to Make Your Advertising Make Money.* Cited above as item 143.

453. Chamberlain, Colin A. "Sales Promotion from the Manufacturer's Point of View," *Admap*, 17 (April, 1981), pp. 174-178.

   Presents a checklist of measurements with which certain sales promotion activities can be judged. Consumer response on four particular sales promotions used by the Heinz Company is given.

454. Dugas, Christine. "'Ad Space' Now Has a Whole New Meaning," *Business Week* July 29, 1985: 52.

   Discusses the increased placement of advertising in unusual places such as atop parking meters, on shopping carts, sports stadium billboards and inside taxicabs.

\*   Engel, James F. and W. Wayne Talarzyk. *Cases in Promotional Strategy*, Revised Edition. Cited above as item 41.

455. Gardner, Meryl Paula and Philip Joel Shuman. "Sponsorship: An Important Component of the Promotions Mix," *Journal of Advertising* 16 (1, 1987): 11-17.

Corporate sponsorships are a rapidly growing part of the promotion mix. The authors survey corporations, channel members, the public and sponsored organizations. The respondents' perceptions of sponsorships, knowledge of sponsored events and behavior in response to sponsorships.

456. Herpel, George L. and Richard A. Collins. *Specialty Advertising in Marketing.* Homewood, Illinois: Dow Jones-Irwin, Inc., 1972.

 Contends that specialty advertising is the most difficult element of the media mix to plan and provides suggestions for its effective use. Included are several short case studies of the successful use of specialty advertising by actual firms.

457. Herpel, George L. and Steve Slack. *Specialty Advertising: New Dimensions in Creative Marketing.* Irving, Texas: Specialty Advertising Association International, 1983.

 Discusses the role and potential of specialty advertising in the promotional strategy. Suggestions for the effective use of this often-overlooked medium are presented.

\* *Imprint.* Advertising Specialty Information Network. Cited above as item 174.

\* Johnson, Keith F. "Cinema Advertising." Cited above as item 396.

458. Kalish, David. "Hitting Consumers Where They Shop." *SCAN* (condensed from *Adweek/Midwest*) June 1986: 23.

 Briefly discusses the increase in in-store advertising over the last five years.

459. Keon, John W., and July Bayer. "An Expert Approach to Sales Promotion Management," *Journal of Advertising*, June/July 1986: 19-26.

Offers sales promotion guidelines for managers of packages goods products. Topics discussed include the value of sales promotion in certain situations, what types of promotions attract repeat purchases, and the characteristics of different promotions.

460. Kessler, Felix. "The Costly Coupon Craze," *Fortune* June 9, 1986: 83-84.

    Reports on the increasing use of consumer sales promotion, mainly couponing, by national marketers. Consumer promotion spending by marketers is increasing while media advertising expenditures fall.

461. Mahany, Gene. *Mahany On Sales Promotion*. Chicago: Crain Books, 1983.

    A publication of columnist Gene Mahany for *Advertising and Sales Promotion*. It includes how to use sampling, refunds, coupons, displays, and other techniques. Details are given on how sales promotion is used abroad.

\* McCarthy, E. Jerome and William D. Perreault, Jr. *Basic Marketing: A Managerial Approach*, Eighth Edition. Cited above as item 215.

462. Narayana, Chem L. and P. S. Raju. "Gifts versus Sweepstakes: Consumer Choices and Profiles," *Journal of Advertising* 14 (1, 1985): 50-53.

    Compares the demographic and socioeconomic characteristics of consumers who prefer gift promotions with those who prefer to enter sweepstakes. The implications for sales promotion and future research are discussed.

463. O'Brien, Glenn. "Like Art," *Artforum* November 1985: 10.

    Discusses the necessities of advertisements for art galleries. Art creates its own demand, and according to the author, the best advertisement is a simple one which promotes the prestige and integrity of the gallery while understating the artist or works featured.

\* Picquet, Sylvere. "The Role of Advertising in the Marketing Mix." Cited above as item 51.

\* Quelch, John A. and Paul W. Farris. *Cases in Advertising and Promotion Management.* Cited above as item 218.

464. Raju, P. S. and Manoj Hastak. "Pre-Trial Cognitive Effects of Cents-Off Coupons," *Journal of Advertising* 12 (2, 1983): 24-33.

Examines the impact of coupons on pre-trial cognitive structure elements such as beliefs, attitudes, behavioral intentions and cognitive response. The results of an experiment with these elements are reported, and their implications for marketers are outlined.

465. Robins, J. Max. "Making Point-of-Purchase More Pointed," *SCAN* (condensed from *ADWEEK*) February 1987: 23.

Discusses the evolution of point-of-purchase advertising into an integral part of the marketing plan. POP has become more sophisticated and more popular among packaged goods marketers. Reasons for POP's appeal are increasing media rates and production costs, decreasing consumer brand loyalty and increasing consumer impulse buying.

466. Robinson, William A. *Best Sales Promotions*, Fifth Volume. Chicago: Crain Books, 1986.

One hundred twenty of the best promotions are presented in this collection. Shows how advertisers make use of rebates, sweepstakes, coupons, sampling, and overlays to meet their objectives. Also see first hand the effects of bigger budgets and elaborate programs have on promotions.

\* Schultz, Don E., Dennis Martin, and William P. Brown. *Strategic Advertising Campaigns.* Cited above as item 322.

467. Schultz, Don E. and William A. Robinson. *Sales Promotion Essentials.* Chicago: Crain Books, 1983.

    Twelve basic techniques that outline a successful sales promotion are explained in this book. It is easy to read and contains the basic principles of sales promotion.

468. Schultz, Don E. and William A. Robinson. *Sales Promotion Management.* Chicago: Crain Books, 1986.

    A great guide on how to put together an effective sales promotion program. It starts with the basics and goes on to teach proven techniques. It also includes suggestions on how to schedule, budget, achieve goals, set objectives and finally measure results.

469. Shoemaker, Robert W. and Vikas Tibrewala. "Relating Coupon Redemption Rates to Past Purchasing of the Brand," *Journal of Advertising Research* October/ November 1985: 40-47.

    Analyzes coupon redeemers based on their ratio of brand purchases to total product class purchases. Also examined are the effects of coupon face value on the redemption rate among different types of consumers.

470. Smith, Frank H., III. "How to Make an Effective Brochure," *Architectural Record* December 1984: 31.

    A marketing consultant discusses the process of preparing a brochure for a design firm. Adaptable to any type of firm, the process includes: individual interviews, concept formulation, copy preparation, photograph selection, request for proposal preparation, selection of graphics designer, and design and production coordination. Each step is discussed in detail.

471. "Special Report: Premiums and Promotions," *Advertising Age* May 5, 1986: 51-533.

A special report on current trends in sales promotion and supplementary media. Articles discuss various ideas and techniques including couponing, rebates, specialty advertising, incentive programs, cereal box toys, and more. Also describes and illustrates the winners of the 1985 Robbie Award for best sales promotion.

472. "Special Supplement on Sales Promotion," *Sales and Marketing Management*, 1 August 1978.

Due to the greater importance of sales promotion and the push for higher profitability, marketers must give more attention to the subject and its long term effects. This article analyzes the topics from different points of view and offers examples of superior promotional ideas used by large companies.

473. Sunoo, Don and Lynn Y. S. Lin. "Sales Effects of Promotion and Advertising," *Journal of Advertising Research*, October 1978, pp. 37-40.

Examines the effects of sales promotion and advertising on sales. Four different effects are studied: sales with no advertising and promotion, sales with only advertising, sales with only promotion, and sales with both advertising and promotion. The author believes that regression analysis is effective for figuring the effects that marketing strategies have on sales.

\*      Tighe, John Francis. "A Good Mailing Needs a Good Offer." Cited above as item 445.

474. *Trade Shows In Black and White: A Guide for Marketers*. New Canaan, Connecticut: Trade Shows Bureau, 1986.

A comprehensive paperback guide to the selling medium of the trade show. Discusses the use of the trade show in the selling process including selecting a show, preparing for the show, exhibiting, and evaluating results. Trade Show Bureau, 249

Locust Avenue, New Canaan, Connecticut 06840. Included is a bibliography of related trade show articles. Free to educators.

475. Young, Robert F. and Stephen A. Greyser. *Managing Cooperative Advertising*. Lexington, Massachusetts: Lexington Books, 1986.

Analyzes cooperative advertising and provides strategies for businesses who use this tool.

# CHAPTER THREE

# CREATING THE ADVERTISING

# CREATING THE ADVERTISING

## Creativity

Putting the message together with the appropriate media requires creativity. How to cultivate creativity is the one thrust of this chapter. Copywriting, layout, physical production, visual presentation (art), package design, and spokespersons are aspects of creativity that are included in the following sections.

\* Adams, Charles F. *Common Sense in Advertising.* Cited above as item 229.

476. Bailey, Harvey. "Deadlines Have Deadening Effects on Creativity," *SCAN* (condensed from *Advertising Age*) August 1985: 21.

    Discusses the poor quality of work associated with hurrying to meet a deadline. Six suggestions for dealing with deadlines are offered.

477. Baker, Stephen. *Systematic Approach to Advertising Strategy.* New York: McGraw-Hill, Inc., 1979.

    Implies that the differences between creative and noncreative are not as sharp as reputed. The author attempts to illustrate creative logic using the pyramid principle.

\* Baldwin, Huntley. *Creating Effective TV Commercials.* Cited above as item 369.

478. Bengston, Timothy A. "Creativity's Paradoxical Character: A Postscript to James Webb Young's Technique for Producing Ideas," *Journal of Advertising* 11 (1, 1982): 3-9.

    Presents criticism of the Youngian creativity model. Several paradoxes present in Young's model are noted, and the author presents arguments on topics such as knowledge and creativity and deadlines which contradict Young's paradigms.

479. Bernstein, David. *Creative Advertising.* London: Longman Group Limited., 1974.

    Offers useful information to both academics and practitioners. Although many topics are discussed, the book focuses on creativity and cites examples from literature as well as advertising.

480. Blasko, Vincent J. and Michael P. Mokwa. "Creativity in Advertising: A Janusian Prespective," *Journal of Advertising* 15 (1986), No. 4: 43-50.

    Examines "Janusian thinking" as a cornerstone of the advertising creative process. Janusian thinking involves emotional resolution of apparent opposite or contradictory ideas. The Janusian approach is becoming more popular in advertisements, and the authors explain many examples.

\* Bogart, Leo. *Strategy in Advertising,* Second Edition. Cited above as item 199.

481. Bonn, Alec. *The 27 Most Common Mistakes in Advertising.* New York: AMA COM, 1978.

    A plainly-written, commonsensical approach to the elements of effective advertising written for the advertiser.

\* Caples, John. *How to Make Your Advertising Make Money.* Cited above as item 143.

482. Caples, John. *Tested Advertising Methods.* Englewood Cliffs, New Jersey: Prentice-Hall, Inc., 1979.

    Discusses methods for producing effective advertising. The writing of headlines and copy is dealt with extensively. Layout and illustrations are also discussed as are testing and elements of appeal.

483. Cilo, Chuck. "Emotion a Powerful Tool for Advertisers," *SCAN* (condensed from *Advertising Age*) August 1985: 10.

    Discusses the use of emotional appeals in addition to the facts of the products in advertisements. Several examples of advertisements using emotional appeals are cited and discussed.

\* Duffy, Ben. *Advertising Media and Markets.* Cited above as item 302.

\* Frazer, Charles F. "Creative Strategy: A Management Perspective." Cited above as item 239.

\* Gross, Edmund J. *Copy Stimulators.* Cited above as item 145.

484. Hafer, W. Keith. *Advertising Writing.* New York: West Publishing Company, 1977.

    A practical guide to writing which discusses the creative process, organization, headline writing and copywriting for the various media.

485. Higgins, Denis. *The Art of Writing Advertising.* Chicago: Crain Books, 1986.

    Through conversations with successful copywriters, the author gives insight into the techniques of successful copywriting.

* Hollingworth, Harry Levi. *Advertising and Selling: Principles of Appeal and Response.* Cited above as item 127.

486. Jewler, A. Jerome. *Creative Strategy in Advertising,* Second Edition. Belmont, California: Wadsworth Publishing, 1985.

   Focuses on copywriting creativity. Writing for print and broadcast media are discussed, as well as layout and design. The author also discusses careers in copywriting.

487. Johnston, Jim. "Decline of Creativity," *Communication Arts* September/October 1985: 24-26.

   Discusses what the author terms a decline in the creativity of current American advertising. Several reasons are cited including the present use of patriotism as a crutch, American provincialism and unwillingness to pick up foreign trends, the view of creativity as a lesser factor in ads, and low risk taking by agencies.

* Jones, John Philip. *What's in a Name?* Cited above as item 50.

488. Karp, Robert E. "Creative Advertising Strategies: The Two Sided Approach." *Business and Society,* Fall 1971: 18-25.

   Advocates the use of two-sided presentations in advertising in order to increase influence and combat counter-advertising. The pros and cons of two-sided presentations are discussed.

* Kleppner, Otto and Irving Settel. *Exploring Advertising.* Cited above as item 308.

* Lucas, D. B. and C. E. Benson. *Psychology for Advertisers.* Cited above as item 130.

* Marsteller, William A. *Creative Management.* Cited above as item 251.

489. McMahan, Harry W. "BST: A Way to Get Your Creative Problems Out of the Revolving Door," *Advertising Age*, June 14, 1971: 78-80.

Discusses the use of BST—basic sales talk in generating new and better ideas for television commercials. Basic sales talk requires the writer to structure the commercial in the same manner as a 30-second door-to-door presentation.

* Mertes, John E. "The Advertisement as Metacommunication." Cited above as item 133.

* Michman, Ronald E. and Donald W. Juggenheimer. *Strategic Advertising Decisions: Selected Readings*. Cited above as item 315.

490. Moriarty, Sandra E. *Creative Advertising: Theory and Practice*. Englewood Cliffs, New Jersey: Prentice-Hall, Inc., 1986.

An introduction to the creative aspects of advertising which includes both theory and practice. A variety of topics including creative strategy, graphics, media and management are covered. Includes examples of classic advertisements which illustrate the principles discussed.

491. Nelson, Roy Paul. *The Design of Advertising*. Dubuque, Iowa: William C. Brown Company Publishers, 1985.

An introduction to the many facets of art direction and design. Many examples of good and bad use of art are included. Local and industrial advertising are included in addition to the Madison Avenue variety.

492. Pake, Alan. "Great Advertising, Made Easy," *Advertising Age*. September 2, 1985: 16.

Discusses the necessity for emotional appeal in successful advertising. The more emotionally involved the audience, the more successful the advertisement.

\* Scheuing, Eberhard E. "Advertising that Sells." Cited above as item 64.

\* Schultz, Don E., Dennis Martin, and William P. Brown. *Strategic Advertising Campaigns.* Cited above as item 322.

493. Sweeny, John. "Assuring Poor Creativity." *SCAN* (condensed from *Advertising Age*) January, 1986: 13-15.

    The author, a former creative director, explains twelve mistakes to avoid in creating advertising.

494. Tyler, William D. "First Rate Advertising Sells Product—Not Slogans or Gimmicks," *Advertising Age,* July 26, 1971: 39-40.

    Stresses the golden rule of advertising—sell the product. He analyzes ten advertisements which do that. Advertising which sells the advertising rather than selling the product is criticized.

495. Vanden Bergh, Bruce G., Leonard N. Reid, and Gerald A. Schorin. "How Many Creative Alternatives to Generate?," *Journal of Advertising* 12 (4, 1983): 46-49.

    Tests and confirms the assumption that the more creative alternatives generated, the better the chance of developing the most effective campaign strategy. Conclusions are based on experiments involving professional creative people from ad agencies and advertising students.

\* Willinger, Kurt. "Quest for the Zap-less Ad." Cited above as item 421.

496. Young, James Webb. *A Techniques for Producing Ideas.* Chicago: Crain Books, 1983.

    The step-by-step process outlined here acts as a catalyst to generate ideas on anything—not just advertising. This handbook sparks the imagination needed for creative thinking in advertising.

*Production*

\*   Alten, Stanley R. *Audio in Media*, Second Edition. Cited above as item 365.

\*   Armer, Alan A. *Directing Television and Film*. Cited above as item 367.

497. Atkin, Charles and Martin Block. "Effectiveness of Celebrity Endorsers," *Journal of Advertising Research* February/March 1983: 57-61.

   Examines the effectiveness of celebrity endorsers in ads, focusing on alcohol advertising and young audiences. Celebrity endorsers were found to have a much greater influence on teenage audiences than in older audiences. The celebrity, however, was perceived as trustworthy by all age groups.

\*   Book, Albert C., et al. *The Radio and Television Commerical*. Cited above as item 373.

\*   Brann, Christian. *Direct Mail and Direct Response Promotion*. Cited above as item 425.

498. Claggett, William M. "Reducing Production Costs," *SCAN* (condensed from *Advertising Age*) April 1987: 12-13.

   Proposes six simple but often overlooked principles which will help advertisers cut television commercial production costs. The focus of the principles is on agency supervision and management.

\*   Day, Harry. "The Seven Deadly Sins." Cited above as item 377.

* Duncan, Calvin P. and James Nelson. "Effects of Humor in a Radio Advertising Experiment." Cited above as item 380.

* Ferguson, Leonard W. "The Importance of the Mechanical Features of an Advertisement." Cited above as item 336.

499. Freiden, Jon B. "Advertising Spokesperson Effects: An Examination of Endorser Type and Gender on Two Audiences," *Journal of Advertising Research* October/November 1984: 33-41.

   Examines the effects of spokesperson type and gender and audience age on consumer attitudes generated by advertising. Likability is found to be a major variable contributing to consumer acceptance of a spokesperson.

500. Gaskin, Malcolm. "Ways to Better Print Ads," *Advertising Age* November 5, 1984: 20.

   A British creative director suggests ten ways in which advertising agencies can produce more creative and effective print advertisements. Suggestions include finding new talent, forgetting "rules," adopting an international perspective, and financially backing good advertisements.

* *Guide to Quality Newspaper Reproduction.* Cited above as item 341.

501. Homa, Joan. "Making Sure a New Client's First Radio Spots Pay Off," *Television/Radio Age* May 13, 1985: 111.

   Proposes the use of retail marketing groups (RMG) by radio stations to ensure the success of a radio advertiser's first spot. RMGs assist the advertiser with advertising and media planning and production details, usually at no extra charge.

* Lewis, E. St. Elmo. *Financial Advertising for Commercial and Savings Banks, Trust Title Insurance, Safe Deposit Companies, and Investment Houses.* Cited above as item 18.

\* Lewis, Herschell Gordon. *How to Make Your Advertising Twice as Effective at Half the Cost.* Cited above as item 284.

\* Lewis, Herschell Gordon. *More Than You Ever Wanted to Know About Mail Order Advertising.* Cited above as item 430.

502. Lockwood, R. Bigelow. *Industrial Advertising Copy.* New York: Garland Publishing, Inc., 1985. Reprint.

    Discusses industrial marketing and how it differs from consumer marketing. Discusses the mechanics of creating advertisements, including illustration, copy, layout, the use of color and the use of coupons. Includes actual examples which illustrate principles.

503. Lowry, Brian. "Clay People Invade World of Advertising," *SCAN* (condensed from *Advertising Age*) December 1986: 15-16.

    Reports on Claymation, the use of animated clay figures in television commercials. This production technique has largely resisted technological advancement, as figures are remodeled by hand between frames. Increasing numbers of advertisers are using Claymation, including Kentucky Fried Chicken and Domino's Pizza.

\* Lucas, Darrell B. and Stewart H. Britt. *Measuring Advertising Effectiveness.* Cited above as item 313.

504. MacLachlan, James. "Listener Perception of Time-Compressed Spokespersons...For Radio Commercials," *Journal of Advertising Research* April/May 1982: 47-51.

    Examines listener perception and acceptance of time-compressed radio spokespersons. Three variables were rated to determine source credibility: friendliness, knowledge and enthusiasm. Time-compressed spokespersons were found to be perceived as more knowledgable and enthusiastic by listeners and were generally better accepted than non-compressed spokespersons.

505. MacLachlan, James. "Making a Message Memorable and Persuasive," *Journal of Advertising Research* December 1983/January 1984: 51-59.

Presents twelve techniques for more effective and persuasive communications in business settings. These techniques apply to a wide variety of situations, including advertising, personal selling and group presentations.

506. McKee, Blaine K. "Readability Formulas Can Aid Good Writing," *Public Relations Journal* July 1967: 8-11.

Discusses the use of quantitative formulas to simplify and clarify writing style. The Flesch, Fog, and Dale and Chall models are presented and compared. An informal survey indicates widespread use of readability formulas in writing done by the business press, government and industry.

\* Moriarity, Sandra E. *Creative Advertising: Theory and Practice.* Cited above as item 490.

\* Nylen, David W. *Advertising: Planning, Implementation, and Control*, Third Edition. Cited above as item 53.

\* O'Donnell, Lewis B., Carl Hausman and Philip Benoit. *Announcing: Broadcast Communicating Today.* Cited above as item 405.

\* Peeler, Bill. "Avoid the 61 Print Ad Pitfalls." Cited above as item 353.

507. Reidenfach, R. Eric and Robert E. Pitts. "Not All CEO's are Created Equal as Advertising Spokespersons: Evaluating the Effective CEO Spokesperson," *Journal of Advertising* 15 (1, 1986): 30-36, 46.

Although there is a growing tendency to use CEO's as corporate spokespersons in advertisements, the authors contend that the CEO is not always the best spokesperson. Several conditions relating to credibility and persuasiveness must be considered before the CEO is used as a spokesperson.

508. Riter, Charles B., Phillip J. Balducci, and Donald McCallum. "Time Compression: New Evidence from an Actual Field Test," *Journal of Advertising Research* December 1982/January 1983: 39-43.

Reports the results of a field experiment to see whether time-compression increased an advertisement's brand awareness, main idea recall and motivational effect. Time compressed advertisements were found to be at least as effective as their normal length counterparts.

\* Rogers, Jason. *Building Newspaper Advertising*. Cited above as item 356.

\* Rosenthal, Edmond M. "Agencies Confront Creative Limitations of 15-second Spots." Cited above as item 411.

509. Rubin, Vicki, Carol Mager, and Hershey H. Friedman. "The Performance of Company President versus Spokesperson in Television Commercials," *Journal of Advertising Research* August/September 1982: 31-33.

Examines the advantages and disadvantages of using the CEO as a company spokesperson and presents the results of an experiment concerning audience perceptions of the CEO as a spokesperson. The CEO is found to be perceived as more trustworthy than a nameless spokesperson.

510. Schlemmer, Richard M. *Handbook of Advertising Art Production*, Second Edition. Englewood Cliffs, New Jersey: Prentice-Hall, Inc., 1976.

Contains the latest information on photographic and printing techniques used in advertising art. It is easy for the beginner or the experienced person to read. Good illustrations of major printing processes and presentation techniques are given in order of production.

\* Schneider, Cy. *Children's Television: The Art, the Business, and How It Works.* Cited above as item 412.

\* Schultz, Don. E., Dennis Martin, and William P. Brown. *Strategic Advertising Campaigns.* Cited above as item 322.

\* Sherrid, Pamela. "Emotional Shorthand." Cited above as item 413.

511. Shuggar, Tony. "Federico Fellini: Making Costly Commercials with 'Il Maestro,'" *Advertising Age* June 2, 1986: 59.

Reports on Italian director Federico Fellini's effort to "stop the criminal massacre of my films on television by commercial breaks" by directing his own commercials. Fellini's commercials are expensive and difficult for advertisers to produce, but his example has encouraged other prominent film directors to make commercials, thus bringing new talent to the industry.

512. Skenazy, Lenore. "Aoki Feeds Advertisers' Needs," *Advertising Age* April 7, 1986: 52.

Reports on the work and techniques of Hirotsuqu Aoki, one of advertising's premier special effects producers. Aoki is best known for his commercials which use animated food as the main characters.

513. Skenazy, Lenore. "Design by Computer: From Drawing Board to Circuit Board," *Advertising Age* October 20, 1986: 52.

Reports on the agency of Dixon and Parcels' use of computer-aided design in package production. The computer allows designers to quickly change package elements and evaluate them. The computer also simulates the look the package will have when on store shelves, thus aiding test marketing. Illustrated.

*   Smith, Frank H., III. "How to Make an Effective Brochure." Cited above as item 470.

*   Stephens, Nancy. "The Effectiveness of Time-Compressed Television Advertisements with Older Adults." Cited above as item 415.

*   Stone, Bob. *Successful Direct Marketing Methods*, Third Edition. Cited above as item 442.

514. Vail, James. "Music as a Marketing Tool," *SCAN* (condensed from *Advertising Age*) December 1985: 7-8.

    Reports on the use of popular music as a tool in advertising. The advantages of using popular music include entertainment value which maintains audience interest and the ability to create an image for a product. Consumer loyalty to a particular artist can be transferred to a brand. Suggestions for use of music are presented.

515. Warner, Lucien and Raymond Frauzen. "Value of Color in Advertising," *Journal of Applied Psychology* 31 (1947): 260-70.

    A pioneer study which compares the effectiveness of color and black and white advertising. The authors find that color's major advantage over black and white lies in its ability to maintain and increase a familiar brand's reputation for quality.

*   White, Hooper. "Ad Groups Analyze Spiraling Production Costs." Cited above as item 419.

*   White, Hooper. *How to Produce Effective TV Commercials*, Second Edition. Cited above as item 420.

*   Young, James Webb. *A Technique for Producing Ideas.* Cited above as item 496.

516. Yovovich, B. G. "Sex in Advertising—the Power and the Perils," *Advertising Age* May 2, 1983: M4-M5.

Presents research findings on the relationship between the use of sex in advertising and brand recall. Four uses of sex in advertising are outlined, including attention getting, sexual fantasy, functional demonstration, and sexaul symbolism. The use of sex as an attention-getting device leads to lower brand recall, but the other uses lead to higher brand recall.

\* Zettl, Herbert. *Television Production Handbook*, Fourth Edition. Cited above as item 422.

## Layout and Copy Writing

* Advertising Research Foundation. *Copy Testing: A Study Prepared for the Advertising Research Foundation.* Cited above as item 34.

* *Art Index.* New York: The H. W. Wilson Company. Cited above as item 140.

* Bailey, Harvey. "What Happened to Copy?" Cited above as item 277.

517. Beltramini, Richard F. and Vincent J. Blasko. "An Analysis of Award-Winning Advertising Headlines," *Journal of Advertising Research* April/May 1986: 48-52.

    Citing the headline as a very important but often overlooked element of print advertising, the authors categorize award winning headlines based on content and approach. Common categories of content of headlines include familiar sayings, contrast, news and information, shock, questions, and curiosity.

518. Bly, Robert W. "When Breaking Copywriting Rules Reaps Rewards," *Business Marketing* April 1985: 118-122.

    A freelance copywriter writes that too often, the "rules" of advertising copywriting are taken as commandments, thus limiting creativity and sometimes, effectiveness. The author provides examples of situations in which common conventions (conciseness, avoidance of jargon, headlines, simple words, short sentences, avoidance of negatives, ignoring the competition, and terseness) can successfully be suspended.

* Book, Albert C. and C. Dennis Schick. *Fundamentals of Copy and Layout*. Cited above as item 373.

* Brann, Christian. *Direct Mail and Direct Response Promotion*. Cited above as item 425.

* Burton, Philip Ward. *Advertising Copywriting*, Third Edition. Cited above as item 203.

* Burton, Philip Ward and Scott C. Purvis, Editors. *Which Ad Pulled Best?*, Fifth Edition. Cited above as item 204.

519. Cafferata, Mike. "Good Copy Is Alive and Well," *Advertising Age* May 3, 1984: M-10.

    Suggests that the best examples of good advertising copy are found in mail order catalogs and gives examples.

* Calkins, Earnest Elmo and Ralph Holden. *Modern Advertising*. Cited above as item 4.

* Caples, John. *Advertising Ideas: A Practical Guide to Methods That Make Advertisements Work*. Cited above as item 331.

* Caples, John. *How to Make Your Advertising Make Money*. Cited above as item 143.

* Caples, John. *Tested Advertising Methods*. Cited above as item 482.

* Christensen, Eric. "All About Freelancing" (as a copywriter). Cited above as item 279.

520. Cowdery, Charles K. "How to Reivew Ad Copy," *SCAN* (condensed from *Advertising Age*) January 1987: 7-8.

    Many times advertising copy is edited and reviewed by individuals who are not themselves professional writers. The author offers three suggestions for more effective reviewing: Read the copy straight through before editing. Check for factual errors. Rather than edit the copy, get the writer to rewrite it.

* Ferguson, Leonard W. "The Importance of the Mechanical Features of an Advertisements." Cited above as item 336.

* Fletcher, Alan D. *Yellow Pages Advertising.* Cited above as item 337.

521. Frederick, J. George. *Masters of Advertising Copy: Principles and Practice of Copy Writing According to Its Leading Practitioners.* New York: Garland Publishing, Inc., 1985 Reprint.

    Leading copywriters reveal in a series of essays the secrets to successful copy writing. Topics discussed include headlines, leads, research, psychology, mechanics, retailing and visual aesthetics.

522. Furse, David H. and David W. Stewart. "Standards for Advertising Copytesting: A Psychometric Interpretation," *Journal of Advertising* 11 (4, 1982): 30-38, 76.

    Contends that present standards for the conduct and reporting of copytesting research are inadequate considering the amount of investment involved. The authors propose a framework for discussion of standards for copytesting research.

* Gaskin, Malcolm. "Ways to Better Print Ads." Cited above as item 500.

* Gross, Edmund J. *Copy Stimulators.* Cited above as item 145.

* Hafer, W. Keith. *Advertising Writing.* Cited above as item 484.

523. Hojek, Frank. "Position Positive," *Marketing and Media Decisions* November 1986: 98.

    Discusses the newspaper layout problem of positioning on a page. Many newspapers in key markets do not accommodate advertisement position requests. The author suggests ways to change the attitudes of editorial staffs to favor accommodating position requests.

\* Higgins, Denis. *The Art of Writing Advertising.* Cited above as item 485.

\* Hopkins, Claude. *Scientific Advertising.* Cited above as item 13.

\* Jewler, A. Jerome. *Creative Strategy in Advertising*, Second Edition. Cited above as item 486.

524. Leach, Kenneth A. "Emphasize the Importance of Quality in Ad Design," *Editor and Publisher* September 11, 1982: 16-17.

    Questions whether newspapers are effectively designing advertisements. Two suggestions are made. Newspapers can redesign their pages so that ads are not in direct competition with each other for attention. Also, newspapers can improve the design of the average advertisement. Several recommended approaches to these suggestions are given.

525. Ligh, James H., and Anil Menon. "A Comparison of Alternative Recognition Measures of Advertising Effectiveness," *Journal of Advertising* 15 (3, 1986): 4-12, 20.

    Several recognition measures are presented and compared empirically and qualitatively. The empirical comparisons showed that there is reasonable convergence among the different recognition formulations. Gives recommendations for research applications.

\* Lewis, Herschell Gordon. *How to Make Your Advertising Twice as Effective at Half the Cost.* Cited above as item 284.

\* Lockwood, R. Bigelow. *Industrial Advertising Copy.* Cited above as item 502.

*   Lucas, Darrell B. and Stewart H. Britt. *Measuring Advertising Effectiveness.* Cited above as item 313.

*   Mach, Tom. "Would You Make a Top Copywriter?" Cited above as item 285.

526. Macklin, M. Carole, Norman T. Bruvold, and Carol Lynn Shea. "Is it Always as Simple as 'Keep It Simple'?," *Journal of Advertising* 14 (4, 1985): 28-35.

    Asserts that the copywriting maxim, "Keep it simple" encourages writers to write at a level below the level of the audience. Reports the results of an experiment in which increasing levels of readability were found not to affect recall, attitude or purchase intent.

527. Malickson, David L., and John W. Nason. *Advertising-How to Write the Kind That Works.* New York: Charles Scribner's Sons, 1982.

    Offers a step-by-step approach to writing for any medium and provides information necessary to produce successful advertisements.

*   Meeske, Milan D. and R. C. Norris. *Copywriting for the Electronic Media: A Practical Guide.* Cited above as item 401.

*   Mertes, John E. "The Advertisement as Metacommunication." Cited above as item 133.

528. Moldovan, Stanley E. "Copy Factors Related to Persuasion Scores." *Journal of Advertising Research* December 1984/January 1985: 16-22.

    Attempts to explain which copy elements affect persuasion. Six elements are identified: credibility, stimulation, tastefulness, empathy/self involvement, and clarity. Credibility was found to have the most influence on the buying decision.

\*     Moriarty, Sandra E. *Creative Advertising: Theory and Practice.* Cited above as item 490.

529. Newsom, Doug, and Bob Carrell. *Public Relations Writing: Form and Style,* Second Edition. Belmont, California: Wadsworth Publishing, 1986.

   Focuses on improving the public relations professional's ability to write for any medium. The book features a unit devoted to writing for special audiences (proposals, annual reports, newsletters, crisis communication, etc.).

\*     Norins, Hanley. *The Compleat Copywriter: A Comprehensive Guide to All Phases of Advertising Communication.* Cited above as item 257.

\*     Papers of the *American Association of Advertising Agencies.* Cited above as item 22.

530. Pesman, Sandra. *Writing For the Media: Public Relations and the Press.* Chicago: Crain Books, 1984.

   A journalist shows how to effectively use various public relations vehicles to the advantage of your organization. Pesman also includes over fifty examples and exercises for improving business copy writing skills.

531. Queenan, Joseph M. "Advertisements of Their Carelessness," *Wall Street Journal* December 1, 1986: 20.

   Provides several examples of grammatical and punctuation errors in advertising copy. The author argues that such oversights ruin the advertisements' credibility and cautions advertisers to be considerate of their grammar.

\*     Scheuing, Eberhard E. "Advertising that Sells." Cited above as item 64.

532. Sibirski, Marilyn. "Ad Doctor Writes Prescription for Effective Print Ads," *Merchandising* February 1985: 68.

Reports on advertising consultant Roger Parker's formula for creating print advertisements. Explains the PAPA (Promise, Amplification, Proof, Action) method of evaluating and constructing newspaper advertisements. Suggestions for copy, layout, photos, and logos are given.

533. Silver, Gerald A. *Graphic Layout and Design*. Albany, New York: Delmar Publishers, Inc., 1981.

Discusses the fundamental skills of printing design. Modern printing methods are discussed, and illustrations explain good and bad applications of design principles.

534. Soley, Lawrence C. and Leonard N. Reid. "Industrial Ad Readership as a Function of Headline Type," *Journal of Advertising* 12 (1, 1983): 34-38.

Examines the importance of the headline in eliciting readership of industrial advertisements by comparing seven headline types. No single headline type is found to produce significantly higher readership than another.

535. "Some Tips on How to Improve Advertising Copy," *SCAN* (reprinted from *Publishers' Auxiliary*) October 1986: 6.

A concise article offers the following tips for writing better ad copy: Use the present tense whenever possible. Use singular nouns and verbs. Use the active voice. Vary sentence and paragraph length. Use contractions. Punctuate properly. Avoid cliches. Support facts with evidence. Involve the reader.

\* Tipper, Harry, George Burton Hotchkiss, Harry L. Hollingworth, and Frank Alvah Parsons. *Advertising, Its Principles and Practices*. Cited above as item 224.

\* Wainwright, Charles Anthony. *The Television Copywriter: How to Create Successful TV Commercials.* Cited above as item 417.

536. Wasserman, Dick. *How to Get Your First Copywriting Job.* New York: Center for Advancement of Advertising, 1985.

    A handbook for beginners which contains suggestions for creating, writing and evaluating copy. Offers advice on getting a job and avoiding common mistakes.

\* Wheeler, Elmer. *Tested Sentences That Sell.* Cited above as item 29.

537. Winke, Jeffery. "The Haiku of Advertising," *Advertising Age,* July 29, 1985: 20-22.

    Compares the poetic form of haiku to advertising copy, drawing an analogy between the two. Conventions common to both include brevity and impact.

## Art and Visual

* *Art Direction.* New York: Advertising Trade Publications, Inc., 1949-present. Cited above as item 164.

* Blonsky, Marshall. "Photographers Focus on the Image." Cited above as item 278.

* "Color in Advertising." Cited above as item 333.

* *Communication Arts.* Palo Alto, California: Coyne and Blanchard, Inc., 1958-present.

    A highly illustrated magazine published eight times a year which is devoted to the commercial visual arts. Cited above as item 168.

* "Communication Arts 1985 Photography Annual." Cited above as item 281.

538. Enrico, Dottie. "Warhol Leaves Mark on Advertising," *SCAN* (condensed from *ADWEEK*) April 1987: 2-3.

    Discusses the advertising legacy left behind by pop artist Andy Warhol. Warhol, best known for his paintings of Campbell's Soup cans, was an innovative advertising artist.

539. Feasley, Florence G. "Television Commercials: The 'Unpopular Art,'" *Journal of Advertising* 13 (1, 1984): 4-10.

    Debates whether the television commercial may rightly be considered art. The definition and functions of art are considered and applied to the television commercial. Commercials are examined with respect to their nature and the nature of art, limitations, the parallel between painting and producing commercials, and other topics.

540. Freeman, Laurie. "Corporate Colors Going 'Hue-Whee!,'" *Advertising Age* May 30, 1985: 3.

Reports on the increased use of non-traditional colors in corporate logos. Bright colors, rather than the standard red or deep blue, are increasing in popularity. This trend is attributed to an improved color watching system called Pantone.

* Henderson, Sally and Robert Landace. *Billboard Art*. Cited above as item 429.

541. Homer, Pamela M. and Lynn R. Kahle. "A Social Adaptation Explanation of the Effects of Surrealism on Advertising," *Journal of Advertising* 15 (2, 1986): 50-54, 60.

Examines the proliferation of surrealism in advertising, especially print advertising. Surrealism and priming are studied within a social adaptation context. The authors call for further research in this topic.

* Kalish, David. "Baby Talk." Cited above as item 283.

542. Kisielius, Jolita and Brianh Sternthal. "Examining the Vividness Controversy: An Availability-Valence Interpretation," *Journal of Consumer Research* 12 (1986): 418-431.

Examines the effects of vividness in advertising information and illustration on consumer attitudes. An availability-valence model is proposed which predicts and explains the effects of vividness.

543. Mills, Kenneth H. and Judith E. Paul. *Applied Visual Merchandising*. Englewood Cliffs, New Jersey: Prentice-Hall, Inc., 1982.

Provides an introduction to the principles of design and arrangement of visual merchandising, focusing on in-store displays and promotions. The elements of color, lighting and arrangement are discussed in depth, as are common errors in display. Industrial display and sign making techniques are also examined. Illustrated.

\* Nelson, Roy Paul. *The Design of Advertising*, Fifth Edition. Cited above as item 491.

544. "No, But I Did See the Movie Poster." *SCAN* December 1985: 10-11.

    Discusses the popularity of movie posters as *objets d'art*. Originally designed as advertising tools, posters which have taken on art status command prices as high as $50,000 from collectors.

545. "*Print*'s Regional Design Annual 1986," *Print* July-August 1986.

    This annual issue illustrates thousands of print advertisements, illustrations, photographs and covers which have artistic quality in their design. Exhibits are arranged by geographic region.

\* Schlemmer, Richard M. *Handbook of Advertising Art Production*, Second Edition. Cited above as item 510.

\* Silver, Gerald A. *Graphic Layout and Design*. Cited above as item 533.

\* "That Touch of...Class." Cited above as item 287.

\* Warner, Lucien and Raymond Frauzen. "Value of Color in Advertising." Cited above as item 515.

\* Weisberger, Fran. "Technological Advancements in Newspapers." Cited above as item 360.

# CHAPTER FOUR

# SPECIAL TYPES OF ADVERTISING

# SPECIAL TYPES OF ADVERTISING

Other areas that are important are in such specialized areas as local (retail) advertising, corporate advertising, public relations and publicity advertising, non-commercial advertising, and political advertising. International advertising, professional and services advertising are other areas that are covered. Of course, there are a few classic articles and books that have proved over time to be of value to the advertiser.

## *Local Advertising*

Local advertising, as opposed to regional or national advertising, refers to advertising within a particular city or county area. Quite often local advertising is referred to as "retail" advertising because local advertising is often preferred by retail stores. References include small business advertising, yellow-page advertising, cooperative advertising, small budget strategies, and techniques unique to retailing advertising in general.

546. Allen, Bonnie. "Advertising for the Small Business: When, Where and How Much?" *Black Enterprise* May 1978: 25-27, 48.

Allen interviews several small business advertising experts who discuss the necessity for small businesses to advertise. Many of these small businesses are retailers. Small budget strategies are discussed for various media.

\* "Best of Class: NORMA Ad Winners," (Retail Advertising). Cited above as item 330.

547. Brannen, William H. *Successful Marketing for Your Small Business.* Englewood Cliffs, New Jersey: Prentice-Hall, Inc., 1978.

A handbook for small business marketing. Includes two chapters on promotion strategy which discuss advertisements, media, planning, evaluation and many other topics related to small business and local advertising.

548. Burton, Philip Ward. *Retail Advertising for the Small Store.* New York: Prentice-Hall, Inc., 1951.

One of the early works on advertising for the small retailer, the book discusses in detail the planning and production of advertising campaigns. The limited resources of a small firm are considered throughout.

549. "Combat On-Again, Off Again Seasonal Business with Creative Promotions," *Independent Restaurants,* February 1986: 54-55.

Advocates advertising to local customers in order to beat seasonality. Methods suggested include frequency promotions, employee sales incentives, bargain-basement media, cross promotions and down-time mailing to regular customers.

550. "Co-op Advertising," *Advertising Age,* 52 (August 17, 1981): 51-516.

A section of this issue discusses the advantages of co-operative advertising and how it improves co-op advertising in each medium. The FTC rules and guidelines for co-op advertising are also discussed.

551. Dean, Sandra Linville. *How to Advertise: A Handbook for Small Business.* Wilmington, Delaware: Enterprise Publishing, Inc., 1980.

   A good manual for the emerging or established firm. Dean explains the benefits of advertising and then begins a stepwise discussion of how to promote the small business. Chapters discuss creating an image for the firm, public relations, budget planning, the various media, cooperative advertising, and planning the campaign. An appendix discusses how to select an ad agency. Emphasis is placed on the local business.

\* Fletcher, Alan D. *Yellow Pages Advertising.* Cited above as item 337.

\* Jackson, Ralph W. and A. Parasuraman. "The Yellow Pages as an Advertising Tool for Small Business." Cited above as item 345.

552. Lader, Martin. "For Small and Mid-Sized Retailers Vendor Dollars Provide the Lever," *Sales and Marketing Management* May 1986: 111-13.

   Discusses retailers' use of cooperative funding for local advertisements. Explains why cooperative advertising is popular with retailers and gives guidelines for media representatives to follow when setting up a vendor support cooperative program for a small or mid-sized retailer.

553. Fuller, Charles. "Advertising on a Shoestring," *Entrepreneur* September 1986: 58-61.

   Fuller interviews advertising executive Allen Zucherman, who gives insights and suggestions for effective small business advertisements. Word of mouth, in store advertising and employee incentive programs are mentioned.

* Hall, S. Roland. *Retail Advertising and Selling.* Cited above as item 342.

* Kalish, David. "Hitting Consumers Where They Shop." Cited above as item 458.

554. Mancini, Robert A. "The Case for Localizing National Media," *Marketing and Media Decisions* May 1984: 176-82.

    Contends that national advertising campaigns often ignore local marketing problems and the opportunities offered by regional media. Local problems may be overcome by integrating local media opportunities into the national campaign.

* Mills, Kenneth H. and Judith E. Paul. *Applied Visual Merchandising.* Cited above as item 543.

* Nelson, Roy Paul. *The Design of Advertising.* Cited above as item 491.

* Norris, James S. *Advertising*, Third Edition. Cited above as item 217.

* Padley, Martin. "How Do You Use Radio—for Price, Event, or Image?" Cited above as item 407.

555. Ross, Stewart Halsey. *The Management of Business-to-Business Advertising: A Working Guide for Small to Mid-Size Companies.* Westport, Connecticut: Quorum Books, 1986.

    A comprehensive and up-to-date guide to advertising and selling to businesses. Taking a pragmatic approach, the guide provides in-depth coverage of the marketing communications process. Working with outside agencies and setting up an in-house advertising facility are discussed.

556. Siegel, Gonnie McClung. *How to Advertise and Promote Your Small Business.* New York: John Wiley and Sons, Inc., 1978.

Stresses simplicity as the important element in promoting a small business. Several topics are discussed in depth, including business analysis, publicity, public relations, media, producing advertisements, and ad evaluation and control.

557. Wantuck, Mary Margaret. "Ad Innovators," *Nation's Business* December 1985: 16-17.

    Reports two successful entrepreneurs' ideas for promoting a business on a small budget. General suggestions include market research, blending publicity and advertising, using news releases, and supplementing traditional forms of advertising with nontraditional forms. The object is to outsmart the competitors without outspending them.

\*   Weinstein, Steve. "Retail Advertising: Looking for a Look." Cited above as item 359.

## Corporate Advertising and Public Relations

558. Ashby, John. "Utilizing the '800' Number," *Marketing and Media Decisions* February 1984: 102-104.

    Offers advice for use of the '800' telephone number in business to business advertising. Business should use an independent inquiry service to handle all calls and also should get an '800' number which is exclusively theirs and can run in all advertisements.

559. Bitter, John. "Public Relations' Identity Crisis," *Public Relations Quarterly* Spring 1986: 12-13.

    Describes problems faced by the public relations profession. Often the organization's public relations person is "the last to know and the first to go." Bitter attributes many problems to the lack of collegiate public relations programs and unfavorable management attitudes.

560. Blumenthal, L. Roy. *The Practice of Public Relations.* New York: The Macmillan Company, 1972.

    Introduces the practice of public relations and the role of the practitioner. Financial, institutional, industrial and government public relaitons are discussed, as is the impact of television on public relations.

\*   Bronson, Gail. "Ads in Movies? You're Already Watching Them," (publicity). Cited above as item 375.

561. Brugaletta, Yolanda. "What Business-to-Business Advertisers Can Learn from Consumer Advertisers," *Journal of Advertising Research* June/July 1985: RC8-9.

Discusses the key differences between consumer advertisers and business-to-business advertisers and the implications of these differences for the business-to-business advertiser.

562. Colford, Steven W. "Deduction Change Could Hurt Issue Ads," *Advertising Age* March 3, 1986: 70.

Reports on the tax-reform issue of restricting deductability of expenses arising from corporate advertising. Opponents of deductability argue that advocacy ads do not aid the consumer and should not be subsidized. Corporations feel this tax-reform measure restricts their first amendment rights.

\* Corbin, Frank. "Ad Agency-PR Company Marriages." Cited above as item 235.

\* Diamond, Sidney A. *Trademark Problems and How to Avoid Them.* Cited above as item 80.

563. Erb, Lyle L. "The Company Publication," *Public Relations Quarterly* Summer 1986: 32.

Discusses the nature of the company publication as a communication vehicle for intrafirm public relations. Too often, the author explains, a company publication is a one-way communication from management's viewpoint. Company publications need to contain objective features of interest to all employees.

564. Flanagan, George A. *Modern Institutional Advertising.* New York: McGraw-Hill Book Company, 1967.

A full treatment of institutional advertising, this book considers how advertising can sell the whole organization in addition to selling its products. Public service, image protection and creativity are among the topics included.

565. Garbett, Thomas F. *Corporate Advertising.* New York: McGraw-Hill, Inc., 1981.

Divided into three units, the book discusses what corporate advertising is, why it is necessary, and how it should be done. Many examples of actual print corporate advertisements illustrate the ideas and principles of the text. A good starting place for those interested in corporate advertising.

566. Garbett, Thomas F. "Researching Corporate Advertising," *Journal of Advertising Research* February/March 1983: 33-37.

Expounds a theory of corporate advertising consisting of different stages. The appropriate research techniques for each stage are discussed.

567. Goldman, Jordan. *Public Relations in the Marketing Mix Introducing Vulnerability Relations.* Chicago: Crain Books, 1986.

Introduces "vulnerability relations"—the public relations equivalent of subliminal advertising as a way for the company to solve its public relations problems indirectly. An especially valuable book for companies which find themselves in a negative public relations situation.

568. Gray, James G., Jr. *Managing the Corporate Image: The Key to Public Trust.* Westport, Connecticut: Quorum Books, 1986.

Deals with the problem of defining and managing the corporate image, especially during times of crisis. Presents several actual case studies in public relations and considers the various roles of management, employees, the media, consumers and government in shaping a corporation's public image. A means of measuring the effectiveness of image building methods is provided.

\*     Griese, Noel L. "AT&T: 1908 Origins of the Nation's Oldest Continuous Institutional Advertising Campaign." Cited above as item 10.

569. Harris, James. "How to Get the Most out of a News Conference," *Public Relations Journal* September 1986: 33-34.

 Explains fourteen tips for insuring the success of a news conference. Emphasis is placed on maximizing media appeal while holding down costs, thus enabling small to medium-sized firms to compete with larger firms for exposure.

570. Hart, Norman A. "Industrial Press Advertising," *Quarterly Review of Marketing*, Spring 1978: 14-16.

 Industrial advertising is discussed considering such elements as market size, market impact potential, selling message, cost, speed of conveying the message, and penetration of the market. The increasing cost of the sales call is illustrated.

571. Hattal, Alvin M. "Checklist: Setting Up a News Conference," *Public Relations Journal* May 1985: 34.

 A public relations professional provides a comprehensive checklist to aid in organizing media and other details of a press conference. Details include preliminaries, briefing the spokesperson, physical arrangements, press releases, the conference, and follow-up.

572. Heath, Robert L. and Richard Alan Nelson. "Image and Issue Advertising: A Corporate and Public Policy Perspective," *Journal of Marketing* Spring 1985: 58-68.

 Reviews current case law and statutes regarding corporate advocacy advertising on controversial issues. The authors offer several guidelines for the corporate communication manager to use in producing advertisements in light of this regulation.

\* "Hints on Getting More Free Publicity" (in radio). Cited above as item 392.

573. Keim, Gerald and Valerie Zeithaml. "Improving the Return on Advocacy Advertising," *Financial Executive* 49 (November 1981): 40-44.

    Examines the rationale of advertising which attempts to "set the record straight" on public issues. The authors cite reasons for ineffectiveness of such advertising and suggest more direct and efficient methods for molding public opinion.

574. Kurzbard, Gary. *Ethos and Industry: A Critical Study of Oil Industry Advertising from 1974-1984.* Ph.D. dissertation. Purdue University, 1984.

    Examines the advocacy advertising of the oil industry during the years 1974-84. The study contends that the industry, faced with increased regulation during a period of gasoline shortages and rising profits, used advertising to mold favorable opinion and avoid increased regulation.

\* Lewis, E. St. Elmo. *Financial Advertising, for Commercial and Savings Banks, Trust Title Insurance, and Safe Deposit Companies, Investment Houses.* Cited above as item 18.

\* Lockwood, R. Bigelow. *Industrial Advertising Copy.* Cited above as item 502.

\* Moore, H. Frazier. *Public Relations: Principles, Cases, and Problems*, Eighth Edition. Cited above as item 216.

\* Nelson, Roy Paul. *The Design of Advertising.* Cited above as item 491.

\* Newsom, Doug and Bob Carrell. *Public Relations Writing: Form and Style*, Second Edition. Cited above as item 529.

575. Newsom, Doug and Alan Scott. *This Is PR: The Realities of Public Relations*, Third Edition. Belmont, California: Wadsworth Publishing, 1985.

A comprehensive guide to current public relations theory and practice, this book includes units on research, audiences, communications theories and channels, and the legal and ethical environment.

576. Patti, Charles H. and John P. McDonald. "Corporate Advertising: Process, Practices and Perspectives (1970-1989)," *Journal of Advertising* 14 (1, 1985): 42-49.

Reports on the corporate advertising practices of 800 of the largest firms in the U.S. Several key issues for management, including the definition of corporate advertising, objectives and measurement, funding and future directions.

\* Pesman, Sandra. *Writing for the Media: Public Relations and the Press*. Cited above as item 530.

577. Pincus, Theodore. "How to Boost Your P/E Multiple," *Fortune* November 10, 1986: 183-186.

Many corporations spend millions on public relations but are very reluctant to make public forecasts or announce business plans. The author argues that this type of information is what many analysts and investors are interested in, and if this information is provided through public relations, a firm's stock price will rise. Specific cases are discussed.

578. Poppe, Fred C. *The 100 Greatest Corporate and Industrial Ads*. New York: Van Nostrand Reinhold Company, Inc., 1983.

A two-page spread is devoted to each of 100 print advertisements for American firms. Each full-size reproduction of a corporate ad is explained by a few accompanying paragraphs. A wide variety of industries are represented.

* Quelch, John A., and Paul W. Farris. *Cases in Advertising and Promotion Management*. Cited above as item 218.

579. Radsch, Robert W. "Business-to-Business Television," *Public Relations Journal* November 1986: 21.

    Reports on the increased use of private cable television networks such as Institutional Research Network by corporations for investor relations. Such media are used to broadcast meetings and special announcements to institutional investors and analysts.

* Ross, Stewart Halsey. *The Management of Business-to-Business Advertising: A Working Guide for Small to Mid-Size Companies*. Cited above as item 555.

* Serafin, Raymond. "Where Rubber Meets the Air." Cited above as item 437.

580. Schonfeld, Eugene P. and John H. Boyd. "The Financial Payoff in Corporate Advertising," *Journal of Advertising Research* February/March 1982: 45-55.

    The authors seek a justification for corporate advertising expenditures by taking a financial portfolio approach. Assuming that the purpose of management is to maximize shareholder wealth, a model describing the relationship between corporate advertising and common stock price is proposed.

* Simon, Raymond. *Publicity and PR Worktext*, Fourth Edition. Cited above as item 221.

* Soley, Lawrence C. and Leonard N. Reid. "Industrial Ad Readership as a Function of Headline Type." Cited above as item 534.

581. Turk, Judy Van Slyke. "Forecasting Tomorrow's Public Relations," *Public Relations Review* Fall 1986: 12-21.

Discusses the necessity for futures research in the public relations field. The nature of forecasting as it relates to public relations planning is covered. Four techniques of futures research are explained, including scanning, trend extrapolation, Delphi, and scenario building.

582. Weir, Walter. "Corporate Advertising from Here On," *Public Relations Journal*, October 1968: 22-24.

    Considers the historical aspects of corporate and public relations advertising. Also discussed are some likely future directions of corporate advertising. The author feels that individuals look at private institutions instead of the government to solve society's problems, therefore the firm should place more emphasis on educating the public on the firm's society contributions.

583. Winters, Lewis C. "The Effect of Brand Advertising on Company Image: Implications for Corporate Advertising," *Journal of Advertising Research* April/May 1986: 54-59.

    Discusses the relationship between brand advertising and corporate advertising, focusing mainly on the oil industry. Finds that corporate advertising can motivate consumers to buy a firm's brands and conversely, brand advertising can positively impact a firm's image. Several suggestions are made for effective corporate advertising.

584. Zenter, Rene D. "Measuring the Effectiveness of Corporate Advertising," *Public Relations Journal*, 34 (November 1978): 24-25.

    Shell Oil provides an example of using survey research to develop and assess an institutional advertising campaign. This article discusses how a campaign developed for Shell by Ogilvy and Mather improved the credibility of the overall company.

## Noncommercial and Political Advertising

Not-for-profit advertising is used in many organizations. Nonbusiness institutions include churches, schools, universities, hospitals, and charities. Of course, advertising is used by such governmental agenices as the military, Post Office, Internal Revenue Service, Social Security Administration and various state agencies. Political advertising has become a big business since the days of President John Kennedy. In this section such techniques as campaign tools, image versus issues, comparative political advertising, and message considerations are referenced.

\*     Barr, David Samuel. *Advertising on Cable: A Practical Guide for Advertisers.* Cited above as item 371.

585.    Berman, Garry. "Mommy Don't," *SCAN* (condensed from *Advertising Age*) February 1987: 20-21.

Reports on the March of Dimes' use of emotional response advertising in its campaign against women's smoking and drinking during pregnancy. The organization's television and print also use disturbing images such as an infant smoking a cigarette to add emotional impact to the message.

\*     Brower, Charlie. "My Life, Loves, and Lumps in the Agency Business." Cited above as item 232.

586.    Buckley, William F. Jr. "William F. Buckley on Politics and Advertising," *Advertising Age* May 10, 1984: M6-M7.

Explains that television coverage is the most valuable asset of a political campaign. Coverage on the news is free and has greater impact than political advertising. The 1984 Jesse Jackson presidential campaign is used as an illustration of using news media to increase popularity at very little cost.

587. "Debating Political Advertising," *Broadcasting* September 30, 1985: 46.

Discusses viewpoints expressed at an American Association of Advertising Agencies conference on whether political advertisements can or should be limited or controlled. The main issue discussed is negative advertising. Suggestions range from making political spots longer to denying there is any problem at all and retaining *status quo*.

588. Diamond, Edwin and Stephen Bates. "The Political Pitch," *Psychology Today*, November 1984: 22-32.

Discusses the unwritten rules of political advertising, which cover topics including advertising of a candidate, negative advertising of an opponent, and image building.

589. Elebash, Camille. "The Americanization of British Political Communications," *Journal of Advertising* 13 (3, 1984): 50-58.

Political advertising has been increasing in importance in Great Britain. The author reports on the current role of political advertising in Great Britain, emphasizing the marketing and communications efforts of the Conservative Party.

590. Faber, Ronald J. and M. Claire Storey. "Recall of Information from Political Advertising," *Journal of Advertising* 13 (3, 1984): 39-44.

Examines whether people can recall information from political advertisements in a natural environment. Survey statistics showed that people recall a preferred candidate's ads more than those of a competitor, but one-third of survey respondents remembered no political advertisements. Recall was more closely related to attitude than to any demographic variable.

\* Glessing, Robert J. and William P. White. *Mass Media: The Invisible Environment.* Cited above as item 85.

\* Griffith, Robert. "The Selling of American: The Advertising Council and American Politics, 1942-1960." Cited above as item 11.

591. Hill, David B. "Political Campaigns and Madison Avenue: A Wavering Partnership," *Journal of Advertising* 13 (3, 1984): 21-26, 58.

Examines the relationships between political candidates and advertising agencies, citing reasons why many agencies avoid political accounts. These reasons include conflicts with business clients and the lack of increased profits to accompany the increased workload. The implications of this trend are discussed.

592. Hill, Doug. "Public Service Ads Seem to Have an Impact," *TV Guide*, April 5-11, 1986: 32.

Discusses the nature and growth of public service advertising on television. The successful example of the drinking and driving advertisements campaign is cited.

593. Hutton, R. Bruce. "Advertising and the Department of Energy's Campaign for Energy Conservation," *Journal of Advertising* 11 (3, 1982): 27-39.

Discusses the Department of Energy's use of paid advertising to promote consumer conservation of energy in the United States. The role of conservation in the country's energy problem and consumer issues affecting the success of government conservation programs are also discussed.

\* Keim, Gerald and Valerie Zerthaml. "Improving the Return on Advocacy Advertising." Cited above as item 573.

594. Konda, Thomas Milan. *Political Advertising and Public Relations by Business in the United States.* Ph.D. dissertation. University of Kentucky, 1983.

Divided into two parts. Part one defines and discusses the contemporary use of political advertising by business and how it relates to the political activities of business. Part two examines the more general topic of political public relations and develops an explanatory model. Konda concludes that businesses use political public relations for combating consumer antipathy, fighting power encroachments by governments and labor and pursuing its own public policy goals.

595. Manoff, Richard K. *Social Marketing: A New Imperative for Public Health.* New York: Praeger Publishers, 1985.

Applies modern marketing techniques to the problem of spreading information on public health and nutrition throughout the world. Establishes guidelines for building a successful health education program through such techniques as target marketing, mass media planning, and evaluation/control. Case studies illustrate proposed strategies.

596. McDaniel, Stephen. "Church Advertising: Views of the Clergy and General Public," *Journal of Advertising* 15 (1, 1986): 24-29.

Reports the results of a national survey of clergy and public attitudes toward church advertising. Opinions about media use, messages and types of advertising are explored. The clergy generally had more favorable opinions than the general public.

597. McGinniss, Joe. *The Selling of the President.* New York: Pocket Books, 1970.

Discusses the Nixon Presidential campaign from an insider's point of view. Includes an outline of the campaign strategy regarding advertising and media relations.

598. Merritt, Sharyne. "Negative Political Advertising: Some Empirical Findings," *Journal of Advertising* 13 (3, 1984): 27-38.

Examines the effects of negative political advertising on constituent attitudes. Negative advertising was found to negatively affect both the targeted candidate and the sponsor. A negative strategy is found not to be appropriate for a minority party candidate.

599. Miller, Annetta and Elisa Williams. "Peddling a Social Cause," *Newsweek* September 1, 1986: 58-59.

Discusses the increasing number of public service announcements produced by Madison Avenue agencies. Several reasons for the increase are cited, including the increased number of social causes, the fresh new creative opportunities of non-commercial advertising, and the public relations value which public service announcements give to the agency.

600. Newman, Bruce I. and Jagdish N. Sheth. "The 'Gender Gap' in Voter Attitudes and Behavior: Some Advertising Implications," *Journal of Advertising* 13 (3, 1984): 4-16.

Examines the differences in males and females regarding voting behavior, intention and beliefs. The study shows that females are as interested and involved in politics as males. Although both sexes evaluate political candidates similarly, the male is more likely to act as an opinion leader.

601. Reid, Leonard N. and Lawrence C. Soley. "Promotional Spending Effects in High Involvement Elections: An Examination of the Voter Involvement Explanation," *Journal of Advertising* 12 (2, 1983): 43-50.

Examines the effects of promotional spending on the number of votes a candidate receives. Senate and House elections are found to be significantly affected by promotional spending, but spending effects vary by candidate type and party affiliation.

602. Rothschild, Michael L. "Political Advertising: A Neglected Policy Issue in Marketing," *Journal of Marketing Research*, February 1978: 58-71.

Considers political advertising from the public policy point of view. The author examines firsthand evidence and makes conclusions in relation to future as well as present campaign legislation.

\* Rust, Roland T., George Haley, and Muhesk Bajaj. "Efficient and Inefficient Media for Political Campaign Advertising." Cited above as item 320.

603. Stephens, Nancy and Bruce D. Merrill. "Targeting the over Sixty-Five Vote in Political Campaigns," *Journal of Advertising* 13 (3, 1984): 17-20, 49.

Examines voting behavior in people over age sixty-five. Older voters are demonstrated to be more Republican and more interested in politics than younger voters. Elderly response to political communications is studied, and implications for campaigns are discussed.

604. Strasser, Steven and Margaret Gerrard Warner. "Battle of the Political Ads," *Newsweek* November 5, 1984: 26.

Discusses the political advertising by Ronald Reagan and Walter Mondale in the 1984 Presidential election. Both candidates spent millions on advertising, but Reagan outspent Mondale by a two-to-one margin.

## International Advertising

Even though this reference book is on American advertising, international marketing and advertising affects the lives of those involved in producing, wholesaling, and retailing of products in America. The international environment, legal and cultural effects, campaigns, and media considerations are described below.

605. "Advertising Abroad," *Mainly Marketing*, March 1975: 1-5.

    Advertising is the main topic of this article on electronic marketing overseas. Foreign editions of the leading domestic electronic publications, multinational and national publications which serve a certain language area are discussed here. Circulation information, frequency of publication, and names and addresses of publications are given.

\*   Barnes, Jimmy D., Brenda J. Moscove, and Javad Rassouli. "An Objective and Task Media Decision Model and Advertising Cost Formula to Determine International Advertising Budgets." Cited above as item 289.

606. Cranch, A. Graeme. "The Changing Faces of International Advertising," *The International Advertiser*, Spring 1972: 4-6.

    Discusses how international advertising has become part of a systematic marketing approach. Ways to improve familiarity and continuity are suggested, and strategic and tactical planning are discussed.

\*   "Dentsu Advertising, Ltd." Cited above as item 238.

607. Donnelly, Paul. "Passing the Test of Good Advertising," *Advertising Age*, January 30, 1986: 11.

Suggests that the best advertising is that which can be used in any country with no major problems, and using this standard, cites examples of good and bad advertisements. For example, ads shown in foreign countries which are produced by multinational agencies tend to be sophisticated, but not as good with detail as those produced by local firms.

608. Dunn, S. Watson, Martin F. Cahill, and Jean J. Boddewyn. *How 15 Transnational Corporations Manage Public Affairs*. Chicago: Crain Books, 1986.

The 15 case histories in this book probe crucial issues (such as dealing with hostile governments) in international public affairs and examine the impact of modern communications and technology on the international marketplace.

609. Eldridge, Francis Reed. *Advertising and Selling Abroad*. New York: Garland Publishing, Inc., 1985 Reprint.

Considers the problems of foreign selling. Eldridge illustrates a variety of techniques and approaches to selling abroad. Advertising considerations are given.

\* Elebash, Camille. "The Americanization of British Political Communications." Cited above as item 589.

610. Farley, John U. "Are There Truly International Products—and Prime Prospects for Them?" *Journal of Advertising Research* October/November 1986: 17-20.

Presents several research findings concerning consumer response to advertising, buyer behavior, and copy research, all in an international context. The author states that while few, if any products will have world appeal, an effective strategy can help a product transcend national boundaries.

611. Field, Michael. "Fragrance Marketers Sniff out Rich Aroma," *Advertising Age*, January 30, 1986: 10.

Focuses on international advertising of perfume in the Kingdom of Saudi Arabia, the sixth largest fragrance market in the world. The content of most ads must be changed somewhat to fit the moral standards of the country.

612. "Foreign Ad Growth Lower Than U.S. Rate," *Advertising Age* February 24, 1986: 52-53.

Reviews projected growth rates of advertising expenditures in nine foreign countries: Australia, Brazil, France, Germany, Italy, Japan, Mexico, Spain, and 174 the U.K. Reasons for predicted growth rates are explained.

\*   Freeman, Alan. "Quebec Law Protecting Kids from Ads Rankles Companies." Cited above as item 82.

613. Green, Robert T., William H. Cunningham, and Isabella C. M. Cunningham. *Journal of Advertising*, Summer 1975: 25-28.

Suggests that it is not good practice to standardize global advertising. A sample was made up of college students from France, Brazil, U.S. and India. It was concluded that campaigns used in Brazil, France and India should not use the same appeals used in the U.S. Each market has different attributes that need to be considered.

614. Greer, Thomas V. and Paul R. Thompson. "Development of Standardized and Harmonized Advertising Regulation in the European Economic Community," *Journal of Advertising* 14 (2, 1985): 23-32, 64.

Examines the development of new European Economic Community directive regarding advertising. The directive seeks to 1) remove distortions of competition in the common market and assure free trade, and 2) protect and inform consumers.

\* Henry, Brian, Editor. *British Television Advertising: The First Thirty Years.* Cited above as item 12.

615. Hill, John S. "Targeting Promotions in Lesser-Developed Countries: A Study of Multinational Corporation Strategies," *Journal of Advertising* 13 (4, 1984): 39-48.

    Describes the difficulty of promotion planning in lesser-developed countries and how marketers target messages in these countries. Promotion strategies for urban, urban/suburban, and urban/suburban/rural areas are compared and contrasted.

616. Hong, Joe W., Aydin Muderrisoglu, and George M. Zinkhan. "Cultural Differences and Advertising Expression: A Comparative Content Analysis of Japanese and U.S. Magazine Advertising," *Journal of Advertising* 16 (1, 1987): 55-62.

    Japanese and American print ads are content analyzed to examine cultural differences. Japanese ads are found to be more emotional and less comparative than U.S. ads. The Japanese ads also were found to contain as many information cues as the U.S. ads.

617. "International Advertising on the Move," *Printer's Ink*, May 13, 1966: 13-73.

    This issue is devoted to international advertising. United States agencies abroad are focused on, and some agency executives from other countries outline their ideas on advertising trends. Also, the article includes lists of agencies that advertise internationally along with their location and key executives.

\* *International Advertiser* (a journal incorporating *Advertising World*). Cited above as item 177.

\* Journal of Advertising History. Cited above as item 179.

618. Killough, James. "Improved Payoffs from Transnational Advertising," *Harvard Business Review*, July-August 1978: 102-110.

Concentrates on the transfer of advertising resources from one country to another. A component of sales success in some countries may be an advertising campaign developed in another. A strategic planning policy needs to be a worldwide approach and not a domestic approach which needs modification for every international step.

619. Liu, Peter Yi-Chih. *The Development of the Advertising Industry in Japan and Taiwan: A Comparison, 1945-1975.* Taipei: International Advertising Agency, Limited, 1975.

Discusses the cultural and economic similarities and differences between Japan and Taiwan, concluding that Taiwan's advertising industry will follow the patterns set by Japan. Contains much statistical data on Japanese and Taiwanese advertising.

* Mackie, Valerie, et. al. "Advertising: Join it and See the World." Cited above as item 250.

* Madden, Charles S., Marjorie J. Caballero, and Shinya Matsuhubo. "Analysis of Information Content in U.S. and Japanese Magazine Advertising." Cited above as item 351.

* Manoff, Richard K. *Social Marketing: A New Imperative for Public Health.* Cited above as item 595.

620. Meziou, Fekri. *The Impact of Advertising on the Less Developed Countries: Some Empirical Evidence.* Ph.D. dissertation. University of Minnesota, 1984.

Examines whether advertising and the promotion of a consumerist society in less developed countries actually leads to economic change. The relationships between advertising expense and economic advancement, economic dependence, political instability and investment in social services are determined. The only significant relationship was a positive correlation between ad expenditure and social services.

## Special Types of Advertising 189

\* Michman, Ronald D. and Donald W. Juggenheimer. *Strategic Advertising Decisions: Selected Readings.* Cited above as item 315.

621. Miracle, Gordon E. *Management of International Advertising.* Ann Arbor, Michigan: The University of Michigan, 1966.

    Focuses on the role of the advertising agency in international advertising. Communication to foreign customers and client organization are discussed, as is the issue of centralization/ decentralization of management.

\* "Murdock's Sky Channel Is Turning Advertisers On." Cited above as item 403.

\* Nevett, T. R. *Advertising in Britain: A History.* Cited above as item 21.

622. O'Connor, James. "International Advertising," *Journal of Advertising*, Vol. 3 No.2, 1974: 9-14.

    Briefly reviews the growth of international trade and looks at the advertising programs of companies like Royal Dutch/Shell, ITT and Gillette. The author makes suggestions for international advertising management and discusses the growth of the multinational advertising agency.

\* Paetzel, Hans W., editor. *Complete Multilingual Dictionary of Advertising.* Cited above as item 153.

623. Peebles, D. M., J. K. Ryans, and I. R. Vernon. "A New Perspective on Advertising Standardization," *European Journal of Marketing*, 1977: 566-576.

    A compromise solution to standardized advertising in multinational markets is proposed. This solution is a desired campaign for multimarket use. With this comes a requirement of control over subsidiareies and a single network advertising agency.

\* Pridgen, Dee. "Satellite Television Advertising and the Regulatory Conflict in Western Europe." Cited above as item 408.

\* Quelch, John A., and Paul W. Farris. *Cases in Advertising and Promotion Management.* Cited above as item 218.

624. Rijkens, R. and G. E. Miracle. *European Regulation of Advertising.* Amsterdam: Elsevier Science Publishers, 1986.

    Broadly covers international advertising regulation in the European Economic Community, and the efforts of business to avoid excessively limiting regulation. The origins and politics of consumer protection activities are discussed. Arguments for increased self-regulation instead of government regulation are presented.

625. Rogosky, Wolf D. "On the Sense of International Advertising Campaigns," *Harvard Manager*, April 1, 1979: 74-75.

    Compares standardized to localized international advertising campaigns. Current approaches are discussed by the author. Also pointed out is the fact that international campaigns are not the advertising directors.

626. Roth, Robert. *International Marketing Communications.* Chicago: Crain Books, 1986.

    A comprehensive guide to international marketing which includes suggestions for media planning, language translation, protocol, public relations and direct selling.

\* Scheuing, Eberhard E. "Advertising That Sells." Cited above as item 64.

627. Semenik, Richard J., and Nan Zhon, and William L. Moore. "Chinese Managers' Attitudes Toward Advertising in China," *Journal of Advertising* 15 (1986) No. 4: 56-62.

Discusses the growth and use of advertising in China since the introduction of Deng Xiaopeng's "market socialism," and surveys Chinese managers' opinions regarding advertising. Overall, the respondents held favorable opinions of advertising, agreeing that advertising promotes economic development and that advertising is a good business tool.

\* Serafin, Raymond. "Flourishing Roman Ad Biz Found." Cited above as item 28.

\* "A Systemized Approach to Media Selection in European Markets." Cited above as item 328.

628. VanDenBurg, Louis. "Media in Europe Is Not Such a Total Jungle, After All," *Industrial Advertising and Marketing*, December 1973: 19-24.

    A summary of media data sources and an overview of up-to-date media practices. It provides a helpful introduction to European media data.

\* Weinstein, Arnold K. "The International Expansion of U.S. Multinational Advertising Agencies." Cited above as item 269.

629. Wills, James R., Jr. and John K. Ryans, Jr. "Attitudes Toward Advertising: A Multinational Study," *Journal of International Business Studies*, 13 (Winter 1982): 121-129.

    Deals with the growing skepticism over advertising. The data presented here reveals the individual perceptions held by a sample of international academicians, students, managers, and consumerists. Managers and consumerists tend to have the most contrasting views, mainly dealing with the informative value of advertising.

630. Wilson, Claire, Tony Shugaar, Geoffrey Lee Martin, and Pat Gray Thomas. "Competitions Provide Creative Exposure," *Advertising Age* December 12, 1986: 22-24.

Reports on competitions for creativity in outdoor advertising in France, Italy, Australia and Canada. Describes the characteristics of the medium in each country. Illustrated.

631. Wood, Wally. "Target: Spanish Commercial Copy," *Marketing and Media Decisions* October 1986: 154-156.

Discusses the problems associated with copy writing and testing for Spanish language commercials. Merely translating a successful English language commercial is inefficient. A Spanish language copy research system which aids marketing efforts aimed to Hispanics is described.

## Professional and Services Advertising

Over 50% of the gross national product figure is for professional and service activities. Such professional people as accountants, lawyers, medical personnel, and financial institutions may now use advertising or promotion. Service advertising promotes those non-tangible products that are difficult to standardize, to store, and are variable.

632. "Advertising," *Journal of Accountancy* November 1986: 98-100.

In 1978, the accounting profession ended its longstanding prohibition of advertising by accountants. The profession's code of ethic now only forbids advertising which is false, misleading or deceptive. This article discusses specific matters regarding the American Institute of Certified Public Accountants' advertising rule.

633. Anderson, W. Thomas, Jr. and Linda L. Golden. "Bank Promotion Strategy," *Journal of Advertising Research* April/May 1984: 53-65.

Briefly reviews the marketing activities of service industries, then examines the importance and impact of communication source, message content and consumer education on bank and financial promotion effectiveness.

\* Barr, David Samuel. *Advertising on Cable: A Practical Guide for Advertisers.* Cited above as item 371.

\*      Beltramini, Richard F. "The Impact of Infomercials: Perspectives of Advertisers and Advertising Agencies." Cited above as item 231.

634.   Benn, Alec. *Advertising Financial Products and Services: Proven Techniques and Principles for Banks, Investment Firms, Insurance Companies and Their Agenices*. Westport, Connecticut: Quorum Books, 1986.

Contends that principles of consumer goods advertising do not work for financial products and provides special principles and techniques for financial advertising. Twenty-four case histories illustrate points of creativity, copywriting, art direction, media planning, and legal regulation. The author also gives advice on how to select an agency with financial advertising experience.

\*      Betancourt, Hal. *The Advertising Answerbook*. Cited above as item 291.

\*      Bloom, Paul N. "Effective Marketing for Professional Services." Cited above as item 75.

635.   Brann, Irwin. "Professional Ad Myths," *SCAN* (reprinted from *Advertising Age*) October 1986: 19-20.

Examines and attacks five popular myths which oppose the concept of advertising by professionals. The myths concern the growth of professional advertising, advertising and fees, advertising and professional success, professionalism and the purpose of advertising. Despite these popular myths, advertising has become an important tool in the marketing of professional services.

\*      Bullard, Jerri Hayes. *Professionals' Attitudes Toward Advertising*. Cited above as item 76.

\*      Cherington, Paul Terry. *The Consumer Looks at Advertising*. Cited above as item 77.

636. Gray, Patricia. "More Lawyers Reluctantly Adopt Strange New Practice—Marketing," *Wall Street Journal* January 30, 1987: 17.

In 1986, lawyers spent $45 million on television commercials, evidencing growing acceptance of advertising by the profession. In addition, many law firms hire public relations firms and produce brochures. However, lawyers who advertise are still sometimes subject to criticism by their more conservative peers.

* Houston, Franklin S. and Diane Scott. "The Determinants of Advertising Page Exposure," (in medical journals). Cited above as item 344.

* Lewis, E. St. Elmo. *Financial Advertising for Commercial and Savings Banks, Trust Title Insurance, Safe Deposit Companies, and Investment Houses.* Cited above as item 18.

* Lichtenberger, John. *Advertising Compliance Law: Handbook for Marketing Professionals and their Counsel.* Cited above as item 149.

* Loesch, K. Linford. "Turning on Radio Advertising for Banks." Cited above as item 399.

* Lorimer, E. S. "Classified Advertising: A Neglected Medium." Cited above as item 349.

* O'Brien, Glenn. "Like Art," (Art Gallery advertising). Cited above as item 463.

637. Shapiro, Irwin A., and Robert F. Majewski. "Should Dentists Advertise?" *Journal of Advertising Research* June/July 1983: 33-37.

Surveys the attitudes of consumers and dentists regarding whether dentists should advertise. Topics discussed include advertising of fees, effect on demand, effect on cost and prestige of the profession. Consumers were more open to advertising than were dentists.

\* Sibirski, Marilyn. "Ad Doctor Writes Prescription for Effective Print Ads." Cited above as item 532.

638. Traylor, Mark B. and Alicia M. Mathias. "The Impact of TV Advertising versus Word of Mouth on the Image of Lawyers: A Projective Experiment," *Journal of Advertising* 12 (4, 1983): 40-45, 49.

Examines the impact of word of mouth and television advertising on the image of lawyers and finds that television advertising adversely affects the image of lawyers. This effect could, however, be effectively countered by positive word of mouth.

\* Woodside, Arch G. and Ilkka A. Ronkainer. "Travel Advertising: Newspaper vs. Magazines." Cited above as item 362.

639. Traynor, Kenneth. "Accountant Advertising: Perceptions, Attitudes, and Behaviors," *Journal of Advertising Research* December 1983/January 1984: 35-40.

Surveys accountants' attitudes toward advertising. Younger accountants are more likely to have favorable attitudes toward advertising than older ones, and larger firms with greater resources are more likely to advertise than smaller firms. The implications of this study for the media are discussed.

640. Zinkhan, George M. and F. Christian Zinkhan. "Response Profiles and Choice Behavior: An Application to Financial Services Advertising," *Journal of Advertising* 14 (3, 1985): 39-44, 51.

Develops a response profile experiment to provide an inventory of possible consumer responses to television and print advertisements for financial services.

## Advertising Classics

As in any academic discipline, there are articles or books that have stood the test of time as being useful and pragmatic. Some of these articles and books are annotated in this section. This is not an exhaustive list of classic articles by any means.

* Agnew, Hugh E. *Outdoor Advertising*. Cited above as item 423.

* Assael, Henry and C. Samuel Craig, Editors. *The History of Advertising*. Cited above as item 2.

641. Barton, Roger, Editor. *Advertising Handbook*. New York: Prentice-Hall, Inc., 1950.

    Thirty-five of the most outstanding figures in advertising's history, including John Caples, Otto Kleppner, and Hugh Agnew, contribute articles to this compilation. Articles discuss practically all major aspects of advertising. A glossary of advertising terms is included and each article is indexed separately for quick reference. Illustrated.

* Calkins, Earnest Elmo and Ralph Holden. *Modern Advertising*. Cited above as item 4.

* Caples, John. *Advertising Ideas: A Practical Guide to Methods that Make Advertisements Work*. Cited above as item 331.

642. Cash, Harold C. and W. J. E. Crissy. "Comparison of Advertising and Selling," *Classics in Marketing*, C. Glen Walters and Donald P. Robin, Editors. Santa Monica, California: Goodyear, 1978.

Discusses the similarities and differences between advertising and selling with respect to communication, perception, thought process, feelings and degree of control. Suggests ways in which salesmen can effectively use advertising.

\* "Communication Arts 1985 Advertising Annual." Cited above as item 280.

643. Dean, Joel. "Does Advertising Belong in the Capital Budget?" *Journal of Marketing* October 1966: 15-21.

Dean, an outstanding scholar on advertising, argues that advertising should be recognized as an investment because it is a present outlay in anticipation of future returns. Methods for evaluating the advertising investment are discussed.

\* Dygert, Warren Benson. *Radio as an Advertising Medium.* Cited above as item 382.

\* Eldridge, Francie Reed. *Advertising and Selling Abroad.* Cited above as item 609.

\* *50 Years of Advertising as Seen Through the Eyes of Advertising Age.* Cited above as item 7.

\* Frederick, J. George. *Masters of Advertising Copy: Principles and Practice of Copy Writing According to Its Leading Practitioners.* Cited above as item 521.

\* Geller, Max A. *Advertising at the Crossroads: Federal Regulation vs Voluntary Controls.* Cited above as item 84.

\* Ghosh, Avijit and C. Samuel Craig, editors. *The Relationship of Advertising Expenditures to Sales: An Anthology of Classic Articles.* Cited above as item 46.

\* *HBR Reprints: Advertising.* Cambridge, Massachusetts: Harvard Business School Review. Cited above as item 48.

Special Types of Advertising 199

\* Hall, S. Roland. *The Advertising Handbook.* Cited above as item 209.

644. Kleppner, Otto. *Advertising Procedure.* New York: Garland Publishing, Inc., 1985. Reprint.

An early work (1925) which analyzes the advertising process, from the generation of an idea to the evaluation. Various topics, including advertisement preparation, scheduling, research and advertising organizations are discussed.

\* Leachman, Harden Bryant. *The Early Advertising Scene.* Cited above as item 17.

\* Lucas, D. B. and C. E. Benson. *Psychology for Advertisers.* Cited above as item 130.

645. McGarry, Edmund D. "The Propaganda Function in Marketing," *Journal of Marketing,* October 1958: 131-139.

Advertising is discussed as propaganda rather than education. The differences between advertising and personal selling, advertising's emotional appeal, and the effects of advertising on media and consumer standards are discussed.

\* Ogilvy, David. *Confessions of an Advertising Man.* Cited above as item 259.

646. Ogilvy, David. *Ogilvy on Advertising.* New York: Crown Publishers, Inc., 1983.

In a series of twenty chapters, the chairman of Ogilvy and Mather discusses a variety of pertinent topics in advertising, including producing effective ads, running an ad agency, public service advertising, the various media, advertising research, and social criticism of advertising. Many examples of actual advertisements illustrate ideas from the text.

\* Papers of the American Association of Advertising Agencies. Cited above as item 22.

\* Perlongo, Bob, editor. *Early American Advertising.* Cited above as item 24.

\* Poppe, Fred C. *The 100 Greatest Corporate and Industrial Ads.* Cited above as item 578.

\* Presbrey, Frank. The History and Development of Advertising. Cited above as item 26.

\* *Printers Ink. Fifty Years 1888-1938.* Cited above as item 27.

647. Starch, Daniel. *Principles of Advertising.* New York: Garland Publishing, Inc., 1985. Reprint.

   A 1923 work in advertising which discusses the human element of advertising as well as technical elements. A thorough, in-depth study.

\* Warner, Lucien and Raymond Franzen. "Value of Color in Advertising." Cited above as item 514.

\* Watkins, Julian Lewis. *The 100 Greatest Advertisements.* Cited above as item 68.

648. White, Irving S. "The Functions of Advertising in Our Culture," *Journal of Marketing*, July 1959: 8-14.

   Stresses that the function of advertising is to modify the perceptual processes of the consumer so that he later views the product in a given predictable way. Three areas of consumer/product interaction influenced by advertising are culture, brand image and direct experience.

# Author Index

Aaker, D. A., 31, 32, 363, 364
Abernethy, A. M., 70
Abrahams, H. P., 1
Acito, F., 33
Adams, C. F., 229
Adams, H. F., 115
Agnew, H. E., 423
Allen, B., 546
Alsop, R., 424, 447
Alten, S. R., 365
Alter, S., 276
Alwitt, L. F., 116
Anderson, R. L., 197
Anderson, W. T., 633
Arens, W. F., 202
Armer, A. A., 367
Ashby, J., 558
Assael, H., 2
Austin, B. A., 368
Atkin, C., 496

Bailey, H., 277, 476
Bajaj, M., 320
Baker, S., 477
Balducci, P. J., 410, 508
Baldwin, H., 369
Barban, A. M., 198, 208, 370
Barbour, F. L., 72
Barnes, J. A., 73
Barnes, J. D., 289
Barr, D. S., 371
Barton, R., 230, 290, 641
Bartone, N. M., 74

Bates, S., 588
Bayer, J., 459
Bayers, B. L., 449
Belk, R. W., 3
Bello, D. C., 117
Beltramini, R. F., 231, 517
Bengston, T. A., 478
Benoit, P., 405
Benn, A., 634
Benson, C. E., 130
Berg, G. C., 35
Berman, G., 585
Bernhardt, K. L., 36
Bernstein, D., 479
Betancourt, H., 291
Biggadike, E. R., 59
Bittner, J. R., 385
Bitter, J., 559
Blasko, V. J., 480, 517
Block, M., 497
Bloom, P. N., 75
Blonsky, M., 278
Blumenthal, L. R., 560
Bly, R. W., 517
Bogart, L., 199, 372
Bolen, W. H., 200
Bonn, A., 481
Book, A. C., 201, 373
Bordon, N. H., 59
Bovie, C. L., 202
Bowman, R., 450, 451
Boyd, H. W., 37
Boyd, J. H., 580

Brann, C. 425
Brann, I., 635
Brannen, W. H., 547
Britt, S. H., 313
Bronson, G., 375
Brower, C., 232
Brown, W. F., 322
Brugaletta, Y., 561
Bruvold, N. T., 526
Buckley, W. F., 586
Bullard, J. H., 76
Burton, P. W., 38, 203, 204, 205, 548
Bush, A. J., 293
Buxton, 233

Caballero, A. E., 79, 137
Cafferata, M., 519
Cagley, J. W., 234
Calkins, E. E., 4
Cannon, H. M., 294, 295, 296, 297
Caples, J., 143, 331, 482
Carrell, B., 529
Cash, H. C., 642
Chamberlain, C. A., 453
Chandon, J., 298
Chapman, B., 332
Cherington, P. T., 77
Christensen, E., 279
Cilo, C., 483
Claggett, W. M., 498
Claus, K. E., 426
Claus, R. J., 426
Clayton, E. R., 299
Cohen, D., 5, 78
Colford, S. W., 562
Collins, R. A., 456
Console, J., 334
Cook. H. R., 300
Corbin, F., 235
Courtney, A. E., 79, 137
Cowdery, C. K., 520

Craig, C. S., 2, 46, 119, 301
Cranch, A. G., 606
Crawford, J. W., 206
Crippen, J. K., 427
Crissy, W. J. E., 642
Cristol, S. M., 198
Crosier, K., 120
Cummings, B., 236
Cummings, B. A., 237
Cunningham, D. R., 210

Darpetti, A., 376
Day, H., 377
Dean, J., 643
Dean, S. L., 551
Debevec, K., 121
Delozier, M. W., 207
Demkowych, C., 378
Diamond, E., 588
Diamond, S. A., 80
Dichter, E., 122
Dirksen, C. J., 39
Dominick, J. R., 329
Donious, J. F., 379
Donnelly, P., 607
Duffy, B., 302
Dugas, C., 454
Duetsch, L. L., 40
Duncan, C. P., 380
Dunlap. W. H., 381
Dunn, S. W., 208, 608
Durand, R. M., 81
Durgee, J. F., 123
Dyer, G., 6
Dygert, W. B., 382

Edwards, M., 383
Eicoff, A., 384
Eldridge, F. R., 609
Elebash, C., 589
Engel, J. F., 41, 42
Enrico, D., 538
Erb, L. L., 563

Author Index    203

Etzel, M. I., 117
Faber, R. J., 406, 590
Fajen, S. R., 303
Farley, J. U., 610
Farris, P. W., 218
Feasley, F. G., 539
Felsenthal, N. G., 385
Ferguson, L. W., 336
Field, M., 611
Finn, D. W., 43
Flanagan, G. A., 564
Fleming, T., 8
Fletcher, A. D., 337
Ford, J. D., 33
Forkan, J. P., 427
Frauzen, R., 515
Frazer, C. F., 239
Freeman, A., 82
Freeman, L., 540
Frederick, J. G., 521
Freiden, J. B., 499
Freidman, H. H., 509
French, G., 83
Fruit, F., 386
Fryburger, V., 37
Fuller, C., 553
Furse, D. H., 416, 522

Garbett, T. F., 565, 566
Gardner, B. B., 44
Gardner, D. M., 72
Gardner, F., 304
Gardner, M. P., 455H
Gates, F., 387
Gelb, B. D., 45, 388
Geller, M. A., 84
Gensch, D. H., 305
Gersh, D., 338, 339
Ghosh, A., 46, 301
Glessing, R. J., 85
Glucroft, H., 241
Golden, L. L., 633

Goldman, J., 567
Goodrich, W. B., 222
Gradner, H. S., 239
Gray, J. G., 568
Gray, P., 636
Green, N. F., 9
Greer, T. V., 614
Greenberg, B., 391
Gresham, L. G., 124
Greyser, S. A., 86, 475
Griese, N. L., 10
Griffin, G., 87, 125
Griffith, R., 11
Gross, E. J., 145
Gross, M., 88
Grossbaut, S., 47

Haase, A. E., 242, 246
Haefner, J. E., 62, 100
Hafer, W. K., 484
Haley, G., 320
Hall, R. W., 306
Hall, S. R., 209, 342
Harmon, R. R., 343
Harms, J. B., 89
Harper, R. C., 389
Harris, J., 569
Harris, J. R., 312
Hart, N. A., 570
Hattal, A. M., 571
Harvey, M. G., 390
Hausman, C., 405
Haygood, R. C., 126
Heath, R. L., 572
Heeter, C., 391
Heflin, D. T. A., 126
Heighton, E. J., 210
Henderson, S., 429
Henry, B., 12
Herpel, G. L., 456, 457
Higgins, D., 485
Hill, D., 592
Hill, D. B., 591

Hill, J. S., 615
Hodgson, R. S., 147
Hojek, F., 523
Holden, R., 4
Hollingworth, H. L., 127, 224
Homa, J., 501
Homer, P. M., 541
Hong, J. W., 616
Hopkins, C., 13
Hotchkiss, G. B., 224
Hotten, J. C., 16
Hotz, M. K., 243
Houston, F. S., 344
Howard, H. H., 228
Hoyer, W. D., 393
Hulbert, J., 90
Hutton, R. B., 593

Ingram, J. J., 436
Iyer, E., 121

Jackson, R. W., 345
Jacoby, S., 346
James, W. S., 395
Jewler, A. J., 486
Johnson, J. D., 14
Johnson, K. F., 396
Johnston, J., 487
Jones, J. P., 50
Jordan, J. J., 244
Joseph, W. B., 128
Jugenheimer, D. W., 315

Kaaty, R. B., 307
Kahle, L.R., 541
Kalish, D., 245, 282, 283, 458
Kaplan, B. M., 397
Karp, R. E., 488
Katzenstein, H., 211
Kaufman, L., 347
Kaufman, L. C., 212
Kaugun, N., 47
Keeler, F. Y., 246

Keim, G., 573
Kelly, P., 355
Kenner, H. J., 15
Kent, D., 247
Keon, J. W., 459
Kessler, F., 460
Kilbourne, W. E., 129
Killough, J., 618
Kinnear, T. C., 36, 42
Kirkpatrick, J., 92
Kisielius, J., 542
Kleppner, O., 213, 308, 644, 693
Koatz, R. B., 148
Kohn, P. M., 51
Kolbe, R. H., 131
Kopec, F. J., 198
Kreshel, P.J., 309, 312
Krugman, D. M., 310, 370
Kunkel, D. L., 93
Kurzbard, G., 311, 574
Kwizbard, G., 105

LaBarbera, P., 400
Laczniak, G. R., 94
Lader, M., 552
Lambert, Z. V., 81
Lamp, E. J., 114
Lancaster, K. M., 309, 312
Landau, R., 429
Lany, P., 61
Larwood, J., 16
Leach, K. A., 524
Leachman, H. B., 17
Lehman, C., 372
Leigh, J. H., 293, 348
Leigh, M. A., 398
Leone, R. P., 321
Lewis, E. St. E., 18
Lewis, H. G., 284, 430
Lichtenberger, J., 149
Ligh, J. H., 525
Lin, L. Y. S., 473
Lipstein, B., 19

Liu, P. Y. C., 619
Lockwood, R. B., 502
Loesch, K. L., 399
Lorenze, P., 431
Lorimor, E. S., 349
Lowry, B., 503
Lucas, D. B., 130, 313
Lynn, J. R., 350

Maas, J., 60
MacDougall, M., 248
Mach, T., 285
Mackie, V., 249
Macklin, M. C., 131, 526
MacLachlan, J., 400, 504, 505
Madden, C. S., 351
Madden, T. J., 132
Mager, C., 509
Mahany, G., 461
Majewski, R. F., 637
Malickson, D. L., 527
Mancini, R. A., 554
Mandell, M. I., 214
Mandose, J., 250
Manoff, R. K., 595
Marchand, L., 20
Marsteller, W.A., 251, 252
Martin, D., 322
Martin, G. L., 630
Martineau, P., 134
Mathias, A. M., 638
Maynard, J., 96
McCarthy, E. J., 215
McCallum, D., 508
McCollum, D., 410
McDaniel, S., 596
McDonald, J. P., 576
McGann, A. F., 314
McGarry, E. D., 645
McGinniss, J., 597
McKee, B. K., 506
McMahan, H. W., 489
Meeske, M. D., 401

Menon, A., 525
Merrill, B. D., 603
Merritt, S., 598
Mertes, J. E., 113, 133
Meyer, T. P., 406
Meziou, F., 620
Michell, P. C. N., 253
Michman, R. D., 315
Miller, A., 599
Mills, K. H., 543
Milsap, C. R., 254
Miracle, G. E., 621, 624
Mitchell, A. A., 115
Mitchell, M. B., 402
Mokwa, M. P., 480
Moldovan, S. E., 528
Moore, H. F., 216
Moore, L. J., 299
Moore, T. E., 97
Moore, W. L. 627
Morgan, E. A., 255
Moriarty, S. E., 490
Moscove, B. J., 289
Moskin, J. R., 256
Muehling, D. D., 47
Murphy, P. E., 94
Myers, J. G., 32

Naples, M. J., 316
Narayana, C. L., 462
Nason, J. W., 527
Nelson, J., 380
Nelson, R. P., 491
Nevett, T. R., 21
Newman, B I., 600
Newsom, D., 529, 575
Newton, D. A., 59
Nichols, L. M., 52
Nicosia, F. M., 39
Nielsen, A. C., 404
Norins, H., 257
Norris, J. S., 217
Norris, R. C., 401

Norris, V. P., 258
Nylen, D. W., 53

O'Brien, G., 463
O'Connor, J., 622
O'Donnell, C. B., 405
O'Guinn, T. C., 406
Ogbourne, A. C., 51
Ogilvy, D., 259, 352, 646
Oshikawa, S., 54

Padley, m., 407
Paetzell, H. W., 153
Painton, S., 129
Pake, A., 492
Papazian, 317
Parasuramon, A., 345
Pasadeos, Y., 55
Paskowski, M., 260
Paslillo, J. G. P., 431
Patti, C. H., 576
Pattis, S. W., 261
Paul, J. E., 543
Pease, O. A., 23
Peebles, D. M., 623
Peeler, B., 353
Peloquin, F., 354
Percy, L., 56
Perlongo, B., 24
Perreault, W. D., 215
Pesman, S., 530
Peterson, R.D., 262
Pfaff, F., 355
Pickett, C. M., 45
Pickquet, S., 57
Pincus, J. D., 114
Pincus, T., 577
Pitts, R. E., 507
Pollay, R. W., 3, 25
Poppe, F. C., 578
Presbrey, F., 26
Preston, I. L., 58
Pridgen, D., 408

Purvis, S. C., 204

Quarles, R. C., 98
Queenan, J. M., 531
Quelch, J. A., 218

Radsch, R. W., 579
Raju, P. S., 462, 464
Raphaelson, J., 352
Rassouli, J., 289
Ray, M. L., 219, 409
Rayans, J. K., 628
Razzouk, N. Y., 343
Reid, L. N., 99, 324, 495, 534, 601
Reidenfach, R. E., 507
Ridley, D., 129
Ries, A., 318
Rijkens, R., 624
Ring, L.T., 59
Riter, C. B., 410, 508
Roberts, C. R., 234
Robins, J. M., 465
Robinson, W. A., 466, 467, 468
Rogers, J., 356
Rogosky, W. D., 625
Roman, K., 60
Ronkainen, I. A., 362
Rosenberg, M., 264
Rosenthal, E. M., 411
Ross, M., 432, 433, 434
Ross, S. H., 555
Rossiter, J. R., 61
Roth, R., 626
Rothe, J. T., 390
Rothschild, M. L., 602
Rotzoll, K. B., 62, 100
Rubin, V., 509
Russell, J. T., 314
Russell, T., 213
Rust, R. T., 319, 320, 321
Ryan, W., 205
Ryans, J. K., 243, 623, 629

## Author Index

Sachs, W. S., 211
Salinger, B., 357
Salmon, C. C., 266
Salmon, C. T., 266
Sandage, C. H., 62, 100
Sandhusen, R., 38
Sawyer, H. G., 63
Scammon, D. L., 101
Scheuing, E. E., 64
Schick, C. D., 201
Schlemmer, R. M., 510
Schneider, C., 412
Schonfeld, E. P., 580
Schulte, T., 102
Schultz, D. E., 220, 322, 467, 468
Scott, A., 575
Scott, D., 344
Scott, W. D., 65
Self, D. R., 436
Semenik, R. J., 101, 627
Sentman, M. A., 358
Serafin, R., 28, 437
Settel, I., 308
Shamo, G.W., 385
Shapiro, I.A., 637
Shea, C. L., 526
Sheffet, M. J., 103
Sherrid, P., 413
Sheth, J. N., 600
Shimp, T. A., 124
Shoemaker, R. W., 469
Shugaar, T., 630
Shuggar, T., 511
Shuman, P. J., 455
Sibirski, M., 532
Siegel, G. Mc., 556
Silver, G. A., 533
Simon, J. L., 104, 323
Simon, R., 221
Sissors, J. Z., 222, 223
Skanklin, W. K., 243

Skenazy, L., 512, 513
Slack, S., 457
Smart, R. G., 51
Smith S. J., 265
Smith, F. H., 470
Snapp, C., 439
Soldow, G. F., 135
Soley, L. C., 99, 105, 311, 324, 534, 601
Soloman, P. J., 118
Sroge, M., 441
Stanley, R. E., 66
Stansfield, R. H., 160
Starch, D., 647
Stayman, D. M., 106
Stein, M. L., 107
Stephens, N., 108, 415, 603
Stern, B. L., 343
Sternthal, B., 119, 542
Stewart, D. W., 416, 522
Stiansen, S., 286
Stone, B., 442, 443
Storey, M. C., 590
Stout, P. A., 136
Strand, P., 444
Strasser, S., 604
Stutts, M. A., 108
Sunoo, D., 473
Surmanek, J., 223, 326, 327
Sweeny, J., 493

Talarzyk, W. W., 41
Tauber, E. M., 67
Taylor, R. A., 109
Teel, J. E., 70
Thompson, J. W., 273
Thompson, P. R., 614
Tibrewala, V., 469
Tighe, J. F., 445
Tipper, H., 224
Toomey, M. A., 309
Trainman, S., 446
Traylor, M. B., 638

Traynor, K., 639
Tully, J. E., 272
Turk, J. V. S., 581
Tyler, W. D., 494

Ulanoff, S. M., 225
Urdang, L., 161

Vail, J., 514
Vaile, R. S., 110
Vanden Bergh, B. G., 265, 495
VanDenBurg, L., 628
Verill, G., 213
Vernon, I. R., 623

Wackman, D. B., 266
Wainwright, C. A., 417
Wantuck, M. M., 557
Warner, D. S., 227
Warner, L., 515
Warner, M. G., 604
Warshaw, M. R., 42
Wasserman, D., 536
Watkins, J. L., 68
Webb, P. H., 409
Weeks, R. R., 418
Weilbacher, W.M., 267, 268
Weinberger, M. G., 132
Weinstein, A. K., 269
Weinstein, S., 359
Weir, W., 582
Weisberger, F., 360
Whetmore, E. J., 226
Whipple, T. W., 79, 137
White, H., 419, 420
White, I. S., 648
White, W. P., 85
Wicko, J. L., 265
William, V. M., 417
Williams, E. L., 49
Williams, E., 599
Willinger, K., 421
Wills, J. R., 629

Wilson, C., 630
Wimmer, R. D., 329
Winke, J., 537
Winters, L. C., 583
Wolfe, R. A., 270
Wood, W., 631
Woodside, A. G., 56, 362
Wright, J. W., 30
Wright, J. S., 272

Young, J. W., 273, 496
Young, R. F., 474
Yovovich, B. G., 515

Zacher, R. V., 69
Zanot, E. J., 114
Zeigenhagen, M. E., 275
Zeigler, S, K., 228
Zeithaml, V., 573
Zenter, R. D., 584
Zetner, H., 274
Zettl, H., 422
Zhon, N., 627
Zimmer, M. R., 321
Zinkhan, F. C., 640
Zinkhan, G. M., 388, 640

JUL 2 0 1988